CONTENTS

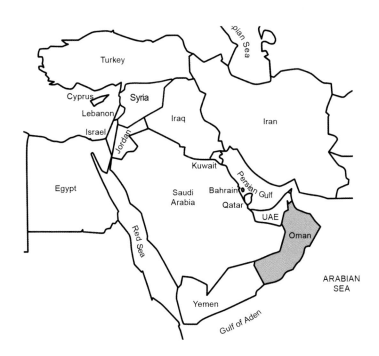

Helion & Company Limited

Unit 8 Amherst Business Centre, Budbrooke Road, Warwick CV34 5WE, England

Tel. 01926 499 619

Email: info@helion.co.uk   Website: www.helion.co.uk   Twitter: @helionbooks   Visit our blog http://blog.helion.co.uk/

Published by Helion & Company 2019

Designed and typeset by Farr out Publications, Wokingham, Berkshire

Cover designed by Paul Hewitt, Battlefield Design (www.battlefield-design.co.uk)

Printed by Henry Ling Ltd, Dorchester, Dorset

Text © Cliff Lord 2019

Photographs © as individually credited

Colour profiles © Anderson Subtil, David Bocquelet and Tom Cooper 2019

Maps © Tom Cooper 2019

Every reasonable effort has been made to trace copyright holders and to obtain their permission for the use of copyright material. The author and publisher apologize for any errors or omissions in this work, and would be grateful if notified of any corrections that should be incorporated in future reprints or editions of this book.

ISBN 978-1-912866-06-9

British Library Cataloguing-in-Publication Data.

A catalogue record for this book is available from the British Library.

All rights reserved. No part of this publication may be reproduced, stored in a retrieval system, or transmitted, in any form, or by any means, electronic, mechanical, photocopying, recording or otherwise, without the express written consent of Helion & Company Limited.

For details of other military history titles published by Helion & Company Limited contact the above address, or visit our website: http://www.helion.co.uk. We always welcome receiving book proposals from prospective authors.

ABBREVIATIONS

AA	Anti-Aircraft
AAA	Anti-Aircraft Artillery
AB	Airforce Base
ACGS	Assistant Chief of General Staff
AD	Air Defence
ADDF	Abu Dhabi Defence Force
Adoo	Name given to the enemy insurgents in Oman
Agal	Camel hobble worn on top of the *shemagh*
Amir	Prince, also an alternate spelling of Emir
ARAMCO	Arabian American Oil Company
Armd	Armoured
Att	Attached
BAF	Bait Al Falaj
BATT	British Army Training Team
Bde	Brigade
BF	Batinah Force
BGB	Border Guard Brigade
Bn	Battalion
BOD	Base Ordnance Depot
Bty	Battery
CASEVAC	Casualty Evacuation
CGS	Chief of General Staff
Chaplis	Sandals
COSSAF	Chief of Staff Sultan's Armed Forces
CSF	Coastal Security Force
Coy	Company
CSAF	Commander Sultan's Armed Forces
DAA	Divisional Administration Area
DCGS	Deputy Chief of General Staff
DG	Dhofar Gendarmerie
DIO	Desert Intelligence Officer
DPM	Disruptive Pattern Material
DR	Desert Regiment
Durrie	Sleeping mat
EME	Electrical and Mechanical Engineers
Emir	Prince (also spelt as Amir)
Fd.	Field
FF	Frontier Force
FFR	Fitted For Radio
FMS	Force Medical Services
FOD	Force Ordnance Depot
FOS	Force Ordnance Services
FPB	Fast Patrol Boat
FQ	Firqat Forces
FRT	Forward Repair Team
FSigs	Force Signals, later SAF Sigs
FTR	Force Transport Regiment
GCC	Gulf Cooperation Council
GHQ	General Headquarters
GSO	General Staff Office
GPMG SF	General Purpose Machine Gun in Sustained Fire
HOW	Howitzer
HQ	Headquarters
HQ MS	Headquarters Musandam Sector
IIBG	Imperial Iranian Brigade Group
Inf.	Infantry
JR	Jebel Regiment
Karlsberg	SAF name for Akut

Katyusha	Multiple rocket launcher (Soviet/Russian origin)
Khunjah	Gulf States dagger
KJ	Kateeba Janoob Oman (Southern Oman Regiment)
KSQA	Koliyat Sultan Qaboos Al Askariya (Sultan Qaboos Military Academy)
LAA	Light Anti-Aircraft
LAD	Light Aid Detachment
LSO	Loan Service Officer
MAF	Muscat Armed Forces
MAM	Muaskar al-Murtafa
Manston	SAF name for Aydam
MBT	Main Battle Tank
MBTR	Main Battle Tank Regiment
MCO	Military Contract Officer
MELF	Middle East Land Forces
Midway	SAF name for Thumrait
MMG	Medium Machine Gun
MoD	Ministry of Defence
MOFF	Muscat & Oman Field Force
MR	Muscat Regiment
MSO	Mudarraat Sultan Oman (Sultan of Oman's Armour)
MT	Motor Transport
MTD	Madrasat Tadreeb A'Dhubat (Officers Training School)
MSF	Musandam Security Force
MUSGAR	Muscat Garrison
Mutarzi	Loyal armed retainers
NCO	Non-Commissioned Officer
Nedg	Desert-like area north of the Dhofar mountains
NFR	Northern Frontier Regiment
NOM	Northern Oman Brigade
NSA	National Survey Authority
OA	Oman Artillery
OCR	Oman Coast Regiment
OG	Oman Gendarmerie
OIG	Oil Installation Guard
OIP	Oil Installation Police
OLA	Oman Liberation Army
OMP	Ordnance Maintenance Park
OOB	Order of Battle
OPR	Oman Parachute Regiment
OPS	Oman Parachute Squadron
OR	Oman Regiment
ORR	Oman Reconnaissance Regiment
ORBAT	Order of Battle
PA	Political Agent
Pagri	Turban (various spellings)
PDO	Petroleum Development Oman
PDRY	Peoples Democratic Republic of Yemen
PFLO	Popular Front for the Liberation of Oman
PFLOAG	Popular Front for the Liberation of Oman and Arabian Gulf
PO	Political Officer
PSF	Peninsula Shield Force
Putties	Strip of khaki cloth covering the lower part of the leg from the ankle to the knee
QM	Quarter Master
QMG	Quarter Master General
Qulla	*Qulla* or *kumma* is an Omani hat, sometimes called pill-box or skull cap
RAF	Royal Air Force

RAFO	Royal Air Force of Oman
RAO	Royal Army of Oman
RCL	Recoilless Rifle
Recce	Reconnaissance
Regt	Regiment
REME	Royal Electrical and Mechanical Engineers
RNO	Royal Navy of Oman
RSM	Regimental Sergeant Major
SAF	Sultan's Armed Forces
SAFE	Sultan's Armed Forces Engineers
SAF Sigs	Sultan's Armed Forces Signals earlier known as Force Signals
SAF Tp	Sultan's Armed Forces Transport
SAFTR	Sultan's Armed Forces Training Regiment
SAS	Special Air Service (British)
SEP	Surrendered Enemy Personnel
SFC	Special Forces Command
Shemagh	Arab cloth headdress worn with or without an agal
Sigcen	Signal Centre
Simba	SAF name for Sarfait and area including Mainbrace main HQ and fire support base, Capstan & Yardarm on PDRY Oman border.
SLR	Self Loading Rifle
SO	Staff Officer
SO Para	Sultan of Oman's Parachute
SOA	Sultan's Oman Artillery
SOAR	Sultan of Oman's Armoured Regiment
SOM	Southern Oman Brigade
SON	Sultan of Oman Navy
SOP	Sultan's Oman Para
SOPR	Sultan's Oman Parachute Regiment later SOP
Sqn	Squadron
TAC Sign	Coloured sign on front and back of vehicles denoting Regiment or Service
Tk	Tank
TNA	The National Archives (UK)
TOL	Trucial Oman Levies
TOS	Trucial Oman Scouts
TOW	Tube-launched, Optically-tracked, Wire-guided (US-made anti-tank missile)
Tp	Troop
Trg	Training
UAE	United Arab Emirates
UAG	Umm al Gawariff. Large military garrison located near Salalah Oman
Wali	Head of a village, guardian, custodian or protector
WBSF	Western Border Security Force
WFR	Western Frontier Regiment
White City	SAF name for Medinat al Haqq
WO	Warrant Officer

AUTHOR'S NOTE

This book describes the professional military and police forces of the Sultanate of Oman, formerly known as the Sultanate of Muscat and Oman. The Sultanate of Oman is a geo-strategically important country as it shares control of the oil rich Arabian Gulf with Iran because it overlooks the Straits of Hormuz from Oman's Musandam enclave. Oman borders the United Arab Emirates, Saudi Arabia and Yemen. The Oman littoral is formed by the Arabian Sea on the southeast, the Gulf of Oman on the northeast and the Straits of

Hormuz facing Iran. There are two enclaves within the United Arab Emirates, Madha and Musandam. Musandam borders the UAE, Straits of Hormuz and Gulf of Oman.

The year 1921 is when the first professional military force was raised in Muscat. However, prior to this, in 1907, Turkish soldiers of the palace guard provided training to the tribal askars who manned the Muscat forts. Internal unrest in 1913 required British Indian Army regiments to be deployed to Muscat to protect it from a large dissident tribal army. They remained there until 1921 when the Muscat Levy Corps was formed, which was the first professional and modern military unit raised in the Sultanate. The military forces have been a cornerstone of stability since inception.

The Sultanate of Oman has been a success story in the Middle East, being stable, economically successful and tolerant. This has been largely due to the enlightened rule of H.M. Sultan Qaboos. His armed forces, based on the British regimental model, were supported by the United Kingdom during the Jebel Akhdar Insurrection and the Dhofar War. This support included many British servicemen with war time experience holding senior command and training positions. They defeated two major insurrections, an attempted communist take-over, and provided an environment for eventual Omanisation of the military and police forces.

It has been a privilege to help to record the contribution made by those who helped in creating safety, stability and security for Oman, and importantly ensuring the free passage of oil through the Straits of Hormuz by their defeat of communist forces during the Dhofar War. For many years this was an unknown war which many now believe paralleled the Vietnam War in importance for the Western world's security and economy.

Finally, I wish to offer my appreciation and thanks to all those that contributed to the writing of this volume without whom it would not have been so comprehensive. Help from veterans of the SAF and military historians has been invaluable as were visits to museums and archives in both the Oman and the UK. Special thanks go to the Sultan's Armed Forces Association who have been so helpful and especially Muqaddam Ian Buttenshaw for his wealth of knowledge, assistance and access to his collection of photographs. Help was also provided by the Sultan's Armed Forces Museum in Muscat. Thanks also go to J.E. Peterson who kindly provided permission to use a number of rare photographs from the Malcolm G Dennison Photograph Collection.

Cliff Lord
Feilding, Manawatu, New Zealand

1

FORCE EVOLUTION AND MAJOR OPERATIONS

Ibadi Muslims established an Imamate in Oman in the year 751 which lasted until the mid-20th century, although there were periods when others ruled. Oman is the only country to have a majority of people who are of the Ibadi religion which has a tradition of moderate conservatism and tolerance.

Trade opportunities drew the Portuguese to the coasts of the Indian Ocean. Muscat, having a fine port was ideal for their use in their dealings with India and the Arabian Gulf. Consequently, Portugal occupied Muscat from 1507 to 1650 and whilst the Ottoman's captured the city in 1552, and 1581 to 1588, they did not retain it for very long. In 1650, local tribesmen drove the Portuguese out and no other European country colonized the area. Many of the

Portuguese fortifications are still to be seen today. In 1646, the Al-Ya'ribi tribe approached the British East India Company regarding a treaty guaranteeing trading, religious and legal rights for British merchants operating in the Oman as the Al Ya'ribi wished to weaken Portugal's control of the area. In 1798 a treaty was signed with the British government, and France and her allies were excluded from Omani territories. An amendment the following year made provision for a British agent at Muscat which created an alliance of equals between Oman and Britain and a treaty of protection. The Sultanate of Muscat, which was a sea faring nation, united with the Imamate of Oman in 1820. Oman had religious imams ruling the interior while the sultans ruled in Muscat and the coast. This union was named the Sultanate of Muscat and Oman, with Muscat the capital of the Sultanate of Muscat, and Nizwa as the capital of the Imamate of Oman. The country, as a strong maritime power, was able to create a number of overseas colonies, and indulged in the slave trade, which provided a huge income. The island of Zanzibar, and the towns of Mombasa and Dar es Salaam on the East African coast came under their control. Britain's prohibition of slavery in the mind-19th century had a highly detrimental impact on their economy. Consequently, many families left Oman, with a large number going to Zanzibar. With the death of ruler Sa'id bin Sultan Al-Busaid in 1856, his sons quarrelled over the succession and consequently the African and Arabian territories were divided into two, these being Zanzibar with its dependencies in East Africa, and Muscat and Oman and its enclave at Gwadar (present day Pakistan). A Treaty of Peace, Friendship and Navigation was signed with Britain in 1891. Dissident Tribes from the interior of Oman attacked Muscat in 1915 but were beaten off with huge casualties and differences between the interior and Muscat were resolved in the Agreement of Seeb in 1920. The Sultanate of Muscat and Oman's enclave of Gwadar, on the Makran Coast, was traditionally where many soldiers were recruited for Oman, but this territory was eventually sold to Pakistan in 1958. The Sultanate of Muscat and Oman was renamed Oman in 1970, with the capital being at Muscat.

OVERVIEW OF MAJOR BATTLES AND COMBAT OPERATIONS

The first record of permanent para-military forces in Muscat dates to 1907. At this time tribal askars manned the Muscat forts and were provided with military training by the Turkish Palace Guard. They wore civilian clothing and were the forerunners to the Muscat Levy Corps of 1921, which was a professional modern military unit albeit small and underfunded. Unrest in the Imamate occurred in 1913 with rebel or dissident tribes taking over Nizwa, Izki and Awabi. In view of this early trouble it was deemed expedient by Britain to send Indian troops to Muscat that year, and an Indian garrison was to remain at Muscat for some years. Initially a sub-unit of 2nd Rajputs, Indian Army, was dispatched from Persia to Muscat. During 1914, men from 95th Russel's Infantry replaced the Rajputs, and troops from 102nd King Edward's Own Grenadiers also arrived from India. This new force provided between 700 and 1,000 trained soldiers to defend Muscat and Muttrah. In support were a number of Baluchi askars, numbering about 250 to 500 men. The Government of India suggested in 1914 that plans should be made to form a regular military unit known as Muscat Forces. This would have been about company strength, but although considered, it was not raised.

THE BATTLE OF BAIT AL FALAJ

In January 1915, dissident forces from the interior attacked Bid Bid with an overwhelming force of about 400 tribesmen, while another group of about 300 men deployed to Wadi Adai. More tribesmen joined the two groups, eventually numbering about 3,000 strong, with the aim of capturing Muscat. On 11 January, the dissidents started their attack at Qurm, Wattayah and the Wadi Adai against four defensive positions located on a high ridge blocking access to Muscat. The 25 men at Piquet Post No.1 withdrew after taking some casualties. Piquet Post No. 4 and an observation post on the summit were surrounded. A counterattack against the dissidents caused the enemy to fall back and they were cleared from most of the ridge, other than Piquet Post No.1, which was captured later by Russel's Infantry. Indian Army casualties were 7 killed and 14 wounded, whereas the enemy casualties were difficult to quantify but believed to be between 186 and 500 dead and with many wounded. The defeat of the dissidents, whilst taking away the immediate threat to Muscat, was a concern to the Sultan and he recognized dialog with the leaders of the insurrection was required, and this led to the Treaty of Seeb in 1920. This treaty was an agreement between Sultan Taimur bin Feisal of Muscat and the Imamate of Oman on 25 September 1920. It recognised Omani autonomy within the interior regions of the British Protectorate of Muscat and Oman, and acknowledged the Sultan's paramountcy. This Treaty remained in force until the early 1950s.

FORMATION OF THE MUSCAT LEVY CORPS

After the end of the First World War, the original idea of raising a force for Muscat came to fruition when the Muscat Levy Corps was formed in 1921. A number of men were recruited from the disbanded Seistan Levy Corps from Baluchistan, which numbered about 250 men, though many fell sick with malaria and were discharged. Most were replaced by Baluch recruited from the Omani enclave of Gwadar on the Makran coast of Baluchistan (part of present-day Pakistan). The Levy was essentially a garrison force for Muscat. Later in the decade an Artillery Section was added, and in 1931 the Muscat Levy Corps was re-designated as the Muscat Infantry and expanded. Muscat and the interior remained relatively peaceful until 1952. All was to change when the Buraimi Oasis was occupied by Saudi Arabian forces.

BURAIMI OASIS

Although Buraimi Oasis is a small area, it was a route centre where five camel tracks met. Located on the border between Abu Dhabi in the Trucial Oman States and the Sultanate of Muscat and Oman (today's UAE and Sultanate of Oman), Buraimi Oasis comprised a total of nine small villages which specialized in date growing. Saudi Arabia claimed the oasis and was supported by American oil companies. The claim was based on raids by the Wahhabis of Nejd who had raided the area in the previous century. In August 1952, a Saudi official with a guard of 40 men moved into Hamasa, one of the nine villages, using transport provided by the oil companies. The Sultan of Muscat, with full agreement of the Imam of Oman, appealed to Britain to ask Saudi Arabia to remove this force, this request, however, was ignored by Saudi Arabia. The Sultan assembled a force of 800 armed warriors to attack the Saudis but was dissuaded by Britain from the massacre that would have ensued. Diplomatic sense prevailed and the Saudis were allowed to remain in situ while negotiations took place. The stalemate came to an end in 1955 when the Trucial Oman Scouts and elements of Muscat and Oman Field Force ejected the Saudi forces.

INSURRECTION AND THE JEBEL AKHDAR

The death of Oman's Imam, Abdullah al-Khalili, saw him succeeded in 1954 by Imam Ghalib bin Ali al Hinai who was supported by

Oman Gendarmerie about 1960. Black leather equipment is worn.
(Malcom G Dennison Photograph Collection, via J. E. Peterson)

Saudi Arabia. Ghalib, who was an Islamic scholar and judge, was considered weak and influenced by his brother Talib. Also at this time, oil prospecting was taking place in the interior with the Sultan's blessing, but the new Imam had not been consulted, which did not please him and his people. The recently raised Muscat and Oman Field Force were also in the Imamate protecting the oil prospectors. Consequently, an independent State was desired by the Imam. While he was not the man to lead a revolution, he did become a figurehead, but was perhaps used by his brother Talib bin Ali al Hinai who did want to lead a revolution and who was a forceful idealist. Nonetheless, Ghalib bin Ali was a clever man and politician supported by Saudi Arabia and with that security chose to rebel against what he saw as an incursion into his territory. On 15 December 1955, the Sultanate stated that it was sending the MAF to suppress a treasonable conspiracy against the sovereignty of the Sultan Saíd bin Taymur. The Muscat and Oman Field Force moved on Nizwa where the Iman's capital and fortress were located, troops occupied the town on 15 December 1955 and Sheikh Suleiman bin Himyar Al-Nabhani surrendered and was eventually sent off to live in Tanuf. The following year, Sheikh Suleiman visited Muscat and was made welcome, given presents, and the implication was that loyalty would bring more. On 18 December 1955 the Imam's brother, Sheikh Talib bin Ali al Hinai, had his forces in Rustaq surrender to the Batinah Force. Talib had previously been living in Saudi Arabia before joining the rebellion on his brother's side, along with his followers.

Imam Ghalib's desire was simply to create a religious republic, but for Sheikh Suleiman bin Himyar this was an opportunity to displace the Sultan's tribe and Saudi Arabia was keen to extend the border in the search for oil. They had more than sufficient arms and money to back the Iman for concessions of land. With the early success of the reunification with the Sultan's forces, Imam Ghalib retired to the safety of Bilad Sait, Jebel Akhdar, while his brother Talib escaped to Saudi Arabia before moving to Cairo. This event was a turning point in the revolt which lead to a highly organised anti-Sultanate dissident movement which was strongly influenced by Egypt and Saudi Arabia. Sheikh Sali bin Issa al Harthi, who was also paramount chief of the al-Hirth, was another of the leaders but with the setback of the revolt decided to go to Saudi Arabia.

The dynamics of the political situation had been altered and a rebellion later took place on the Green Mountain (Jebel Akhdar). Although Ghalib bin Ali Al Hinai was seen by many as the head of the rebellion it was actually led by Sheikh Suleiman bin Himyar Al-

Nabhani, Lord of the Jebel Akhdar, and a descendant of the ancient Nabahina dynasty and, importantly, aided by his Beni Riyam tribe. He was also paramount sheikh of the Hinawi tribal federation. The Beni Riyam had a historical dislike of the Abu Saidi tribe of Sultan Said bin Taimur of Muscat and Oman, and thus encouraged the insurrection against the Sultan in 1957. The tribe was also the biggest in Oman and provided most of the dissident fighters.

Talib bin Ali al Hinai commanded the Oman Liberation Army (OLA), with 300 or more trained Omani fighters, who mainly lived outside of Oman and trained at Dammam on the Arabian Gulf coast of Saudi Arabia under American mercenary instructors. The doctrine of Egypt's Nasser influenced his thinking as he wished to take over the Sultanate and remove the British.

On the other hand, Sheikh Suleiman had an agenda which was more interested in oil contracts than Arab nationalism. The two leaders were able to muster the OLA plus two or three thousand tribal fighters who were in the main Beni Riyam. The Arabian American Oil Company (ARAMCO), always eager for oil exploration opportunities, had encouraged Saudi Arabia to be more aggressive in border disputes, which could harbour the chance of discovering more oil. They were well aware that Sultan Said bin Taimur had only a small professional military force consisting of three understrength and underequipped infantry regiments, due to lack of funds, plus the very small fledgling Dhofar Force. Although the Sultanate had guaranteed the autonomous interior as an Imamate, Sultan Said bin Taimur had always desired to bring the interior back into the Sultanate. The Imamate, under its new leader, became closely associated with Saudi Arabia. Saudi Arabia and ARAMCO were very interested in oil and well aware of the potential in Oman. Sultan Taimur was also aware of the potential of oil revenue from the British oil prospectors.

Another figure in the revolt was Sheikh Ibrahim bin Issa al Harthi, who was the brother of Sheikh Sali bin Issa al Harthi in exile in Saudi Arabia and was in contact with him. Sheikh Ibrahim was at Sharquiya in March 1957 where he planned to start a revolt against the Sultan with about 70 hard core followers. This was to be in conjunction with Talib landing a force of 50 OLA soldiers on the Batinah coast. Talib's force arrived late due to problems with their boats and Ibrahim was obliged to seek negotiations with the Sultan. He was invited to go to Muscat to talk with the Sultan but when he arrived was jailed. Talib was eventually successful and was able to join his brother Ghalib, on the Jebel Akhdar, who proclaimed the rebirth of the Imamate in June.

A major reorganization of the MAF occurred in 1957: the Batinah Force was renamed the Northern Frontier Regiment, and the Muscat and Oman Field Force became the Oman Regiment. The Muscat Infantry was renamed the Muscat Regiment. This reorganization did, in time, put the units on a more professional basis. MAF HQ was based in the fort at Bait al Falaj (BAF) and included seven officers and about 50 men and a troop from the Royal Signals which later returned to Bahrain.

The following year the Oman Regiment moved from Firq, heading for Hamra, to confront Talib's forces. Overnight on 12 and 13 July 1958, Suleiman bin Himyar who had been on parole in Muscat, decided to join forces with the other rebels. The Beni Riyam and Beni Hinna tribes came to his assistance and between them controlled most of the Jebel Akhdar. The Oman Regiment suddenly became compromised and a withdrawal was made. Constantly ambushed, snipped at, and the roads mined, the regiment was severely mauled. Many were killed, wounded, taken prisoner or deserted. Large amounts of supplies and ammunition were lost and

Captain Noel Ayliffe-Jones of the Muscat & Oman Field Force. Note the words Muscat & Oman Field Force stencilled on the Land Rover door. (Malcolm G Dennison Photograph Collection, via J E Peterson)

Two Muscat and Oman Field Force *jundies* ca 1955-1956. (Malcolm G Dennison Photograph Collection, via J E Peterson)

many vehicles blown up or captured. About the equivalent of one company of the Oman Regiment survived and was absorbed into the other regiments. The commanding officer was dismissed by the Sultan. As a consequence of this military defeat the interior was lost, including the important capital Nizwa, Izki, Bahla and the route to Muscat was under Imamate control. Jebel Akhdar had become an Imamate fortress. Saudi Arabia provided the rebels with arms and transport, and Radio Cairo used its propaganda to great effect to denigrate the British and what it called the "struggle" against the imperialist forces in the Gulf. The insurgents had their base within the safety of the Jebel Akhdar; the mountain was like a massive fortress 20 miles long by ten miles wide and about 6,500 feet above sea level with sheer rock cliffs and at the top was a fertile plateau. Talib's forces now included about 500 armed men and at least 150 to guard the mountain.

British help was requested by the Sultan and a force was quickly put together to recapture the Imamate capital at Nizwa and help restore the Sultan's authority over the hinterland. Brig. J.A.R. Robertson commanded a force of a rifle company of the Cameronians (Scottish Rifles) with a cut-down Battalion HQ, and the MMG and mortar platoons of the regiment. He also had one troop of the 15/19th King's Hussars and two squadrons of Trucial Oman Scouts (TOS), the latter named as Carter Force after their commander. Other non-British forces included the Northern Frontier Regiment, newly raised, and a small unit of the survivors of the Oman Regiment. Nizwa was quickly captured without casualties and the troops were joined by Haughcol (named after Major Haugh, a survivor of the Oman Regiment) to garrison Nizwa once captured. When the interior was recaptured the insurgents still retained the high ground of their seemingly impregnable fortress on the top of Jebel Akhdar. British troops were moved out except for the 15/19th Hussars' troop of Ferret scout cars, which were eventually relieved by one troop of 13/18th Hussars, later increased to two troops.

The Muscat Armed Forces were renamed the Sultan's Armed Forces (SAF) in 1958. Britain's Colonel David Smiley was sent to Oman in April 1958 as Chief of Staff of the Sultan's Armed Forces after the reorganization of the SAF, and the disbandment of the remains of the Oman Regiment. British assistance was required to remove the insurgents from the Jebel and Colonel Smiley had at his disposal about 1,000 British troops including: 2 troops of the 13/18th Hussars at Nizwa, 1 officer and 8 NCOs of the Royal Marines (instructors for the NFR), small detachments of various corps including Royal Signals, and ground crews from the Royal Air Force (RAF) of the United Kingdom. Later, contingents of the Life Guards and Special Air Service arrived, and two squadrons of the Trucial Oman Scouts were at Izki and Ibri. A squadron of the Life Guards was introduced to reinforce the TOS squadrons. During November 1958, a patrol of the Muscat Regiment discovered a route to the top of the Jebel Akhdar that was unguarded. This was the first time the SAF had reached the top of the mountain and found a future route that they could climb up with donkeys. In January 1959, a joint operation by the SAF and two squadrons of the SAS scaled the Jebel overnight and took the rebels by surprise. Talib's men melted back into the population. The leaders went into exile in Saudi Arabia and the war was concluded except for occasional insurgents crossing the border to lay mines, which eventually ceased. The Oman Gendarmerie (OG) was raised in 1959 to police the frontier and to help stop gunrunning as well as the more mundane assisting with customs checks. OG was eventually to become a very successful and large unit of the SAF.

EXPANSION

The 1960s saw a huge expansion and a further reorganization of the military forces of Oman. Some of the improvements included new camps, new units, revised establishments, more artillery, coastal patrol, education, more aircraft, more recruit training, and a pay increase to Trucial Oman Scouts levels. The primary infantry weapons at this time were the SMLE .303 rifle, Bren gun, and the British 2-inch mortar. The FN rifle was introduced at the end of the decade along with 81mm mortars. In the late 1960s, the Adoo (or enemy) were well armed with Kalashnikov AKS assault rifles, which followed on from the AK-47 but with a folding steel shoulder stock, and SKS semi-automatic rifles. They also had mines, recoilless rifles and 14.5mm machine guns, and outnumbered the SAF.

OPERATION INTRADON

Five months after the coup in 1970, a serious internal threat to Oman surfaced in the Musandam Peninsula where members of a local tribe were hostile to the new Sultan. In response, Britain sent in SAS troops who were dropped into the area to remove the dissident forces which may have numbered over 90. The operation was successful no further trouble occurred there.

DHOFAR WAR

Dhofar is the southern province of Oman and covers over a third of the country. Bordered by Saudi Arabia to the north and the PDYR (now Yemen) in the west, the diverse topology of the country has a fertile but small narrow coastal plain bordered by rugged mountains and over which lies desert. The capital is Salalah on the 60 km long plain. The rest of the coast is wooded mountains. Both central and northern areas of the jebel are barren with deep valleys *(wadi)*. While the mountains run the length of the province, they are no more than 30 to 50 kms wide with an average height between 1,000 and 1,500 metres and with the highest point at 2,100 metres. Eventually the jebel gives way to the southern peripheral of the Empty Quarter. The climate is hot and dry, but the coastal area does receive the *Khareef,* which are the south west monsoon winds from June to September and the *Shimaal,* which are dry hot winds from the north during the two months of December and January. It is within this difficult territory and extremes of temperature that the Dhofar War was fought and eventually won.

The Dhofar Liberation Front (DLF) was created in 1965 from the various rebel groups in Dhofar with an Arab Nationalist perspective. Mussalim bin Nufal was a prominent early activist seeking assistance for Dhofar province, which was particularly neglected by Sultan Said bin Taimur. The province was culturally and ethnically different from the rest of Oman and the people felt ignored. The rebellion remained at low intensity until 1967 when the Arab-Israeli Six Day War had a strong impact on Arab opinion throughout the Gulf, as did the British withdrawal from the Federation of South Arabia (Aden) in the same year. The People's Republic of Southern Yemen (PRSY) was established in November 1967 in the former Federation of South Arabia. It was not long before supplies and arms were made available to the rebels in Dhofar from the PRSY's Mahra province which bordered Dhofar, and also provided a conduit for new recruits.

A radical Marxist wing of the National Liberation Front of the PRSY gained power on 1 December 1970 and reorganized the country into the People's Democratic Republic of Yemen (PDRY). The PDRY was strongly allied to the Soviet Union, China and Cuba. China had already provided training along with indoctrination, which radicalized the rebel movement. The small town of Hawf, on the coast close to the border with Oman, became a centre for training and logistics. In Oman, the nationalist orientated Dhofar Liberation Front was renamed the Popular Front for the Liberation of Oman and the Arab Gulf (PFLOAG) in 1968 and adopted a communist doctrine. Their aim was no longer the reform of Dhofar but was now the overthrow of the Sultanate of Oman and other pro-Western regimes in the Arabian Gulf. Arms were provided by Cuba and the Soviet Union.

There was also the National Democratic Front for the Liberation of the Occupied Arab Gulf (NDFLOAG) formed in 1970 from the 1969 Popular Revolutionary Movement (PRM). Most of its leaders were killed or captured in an abortive attempt to blow up the SAF fort at Nizwa Camp and an attack on Izki. The entire organization became compromised and discredited, arrests were made, arms caches discovered, and its remnants were obliged to join the PFLOAG.

By 1969, the PFLOAG insurgents, locally known as the Adoo, had control of much of Dhofar, and there were also attacks on SAF positions in other parts of Oman. The reactionary rule of Sultan Said bin Taimur was despotic and hampered efforts to thwart the threat from the PFLOAG. Enemy forces were pushing the SAF back in Dhofar by 1970, the PFLOAG controlled more than three-quarters of sparsely populated Dhofar, and Salalah and its airfield was in danger of being overrun. The small revolt had turned into a major dissident force with powerful international backers and became a major threat to the Gulf States.

It became expedient that a major change was required in Muscat and consequently the Sultan was overthrown in a palace coup, and his son, Qaboos bin Said, took on the mantle of leadership. The old sultan had become an impediment to the safety and progress of the country. This had become a time of change; the new sultan had been to the British Royal Military Academy at Sandhurst, and had also served as an officer in the British Army with 1st Battalion the Cameronians (Scottish Rifles). His modern appreciation of the world, and first-hand experience with a top NATO army was instrumental in ensuring major social and military reforms were implemented within Oman and the SAF. Sultan Qaboos renamed the Sultanate of Muscat and Oman as the Sultanate of Oman in 1970, with the capital in Muscat. An amnesty was called by the Sultan for Surrendered Enemy Personnel (SEP) and many joined the new Firqat irregular units, which included small teams from the Special Air Service for training and guidance. These training teams were officially and euphemistically called British Army Training Teams or BATTs. The successful Firqat concept denied the rebels local support and access to their areas as well as providing irregular troops for ambushing and intelligence gathering. The improvement of intelligence was in part due to the fact that the Firqat were able to penetrate areas of the Jebel that were previously inaccessible to regular SAF battalions. These irregular troops not only knew the areas they were allocated to, but knew the people and customs, and therefore could recognize Adoo from the local population. They were able to win the hearts and minds of the population with state development projects and the medical assistance that the SAF provided, and in turn the intelligence they gleaned from the local population enabled the SAF to neutralise enemy forces in their area. One of the major achievements of the Firqat was their success at "turning" Adoo to fight for the Sultan, using techniques similar to those learned by the British with their success in Kenya and Malaya and refined for the Dhofar situation.

HQ Dhofar Area was established in 1971 at Umm al Gawariff to manage the insurgency. This same year the NDFLOAG and PFLOAG merged in December. Firqah were being raised to complement the rifle battalions and to use their local knowledge and fighting skills in their home territories. Firqat Salahdin was part of a small force that recaptured the coastal town of Sudh from the Adoo in February. The SAF conducted many operations to remove the PFLOAG from Oman over the next few years. Strategic ground had to be retaken from the Adoo and defensive lines were required to stop or reduce the ability of the enemy to simply walk through the rugged Dhofar terrain without being challenged. Defensive lines were time consuming and expensive to build, plus a large number of soldiers were required to protect those building the lines. The task involved the laying of minefields, obstacles, and barbed wire across the terrain of remote western Dhofar. Once built, the defensive line would be patrolled and guarded. A hearts and minds policy of civil development was then carried out on the eastern side of the lines. This system consisted of the SAF moving into areas of significant population in eastern Dhofar, and when established there the Firqat was able to deploy into the local hinterland to ensure the population were not threatened by the Adoo. Once an area was considered safe Civil Action Teams (CAT) would move in and provide medical aid, buildings and whatever was required to provide services for the population.

MAJOR OFFENSIVE AND DEFENSIVE OPERATIONS

While the defensive line policy was critical, as were the diplomatic efforts, the Dhofar War still had to be won through expelling the enemy on the ground from Oman. Many operations were critical to the success of the SAF, but three events stand out and are considered exceptional to the defeat of the PFLOAG forces from People's Democratic Republic of Yemen. They were: Operation Jaguar, Operation Simba, and the Battle of Mirbat.

OPERATION JAGUAR, 2 OCTOBER 1971

By October 1971 the initiative started to turn in favour of the Sultanate forces. Operation Jaguar saw a daring move to capture a strategic location on the Central Jebel. The object of the attack was to make a secure base on the Jebel, including an airhead, and importantly to be able to remain there during the monsoon. Once completed, the pacification of the eastern Jebel could proceed. The task was accomplished with two SAS squadrons, about 300 Firqah, two companies of the Muscat Regiment, one company of the Jebel Regiment, Baluch Askari, support from the artillery, plus helicopters and air support. The AB.205 helicopters saw their first major action during this operation when six were used to deploy more than 300 troops and the supplies of the SAS, the Firqat and other units into a forward operating base. GPMGs and 81mm mortars were made available to all ground forces. The operation started with a night march that saw two SAS squadrons, two Firqats and Baluch Askari reach an old landing strip, called Lympne, on the Jebel. Reinforcements were flown in once the strip was secured. Unfortunately, the airstrip proved to be unsuitable for helicopters and Skyvan's due to it being damaged by the aircraft. Consequently, a move to Jibjat, about ten kilometres westwards, was made to remedy the situation. SAS squadrons, each with a Firqat, swept down the east and west Wadi Darbat, encountering stiff resistance but nothing remained in their way. Having neutralized the enemy, a new encampment was made at Madinat-al-Haq (White City), which was situated on a plateau. Not only was this base a serious fortification but also a springboard for patrols. It became a centre for the Sultanate to help the local Jebalis with medical facilities and included a store and a school. This was a major hearts and minds success. After this, Operation Leopard was able to take place, which set up a line of piquet's from Mughsayl on the coast to the Negd north of the Jebel designed to deny resupply to the insurgents from the PDRY. Known as the Leopard Line, it was later reconstructed and became the Hornbeam Line, which was in turn later replaced by the Damavand Line further west.

OPERATION SIMBA, 16 APRIL 1972

Operation Simba was the code name for a heliborne-aided operation to establish a position at Sarfait at the extreme western end of the coast bordering the PDRY. The Swahili name Simba (lion) was used for the entire area for some time before reverting back to Sarfait. The operation was intended not only to take back Omani territory and to be a concern to the PFLOAG, because of its close proximity to the border, but it was also to dominate the supply routes used by the insurgents and to stop the transfer of arms, men and stores from the PDRY via the coastal route. Importantly, it was hoped that this operation would bring the war to the attention of other Arab states, and Iran, through media coverage, and to enlist support from them. The Omani border with the PDRY was 288 kilometres long and in very rugged mountainous country in which the number of infantry battalions available to patrol and guard this area was quite inadequate. Foreign assistance, in the form of men, helicopters,

artillery and stores was needed to help block the insurgents' routes into Dhofar.

A plan was devised to create a battalion group at *Akoot* (Karlsberg) and send them to capture a prominent ridge close to the PDRY border near Sarfait. On 16 April a Desert Regiment Group along with Firqat Tariq bin Ziyad under Lt Col Knocker captured Sarfait. The execution of the operation went well but the severity of the weather delayed the operation. Habrut Fort sited on the PDRY border up-country was attacked and destroyed by PDRY forces in May in retaliation and as a diversion from Sarfait. Madinat al Haq aka (White City) was reinforced and held through the monsoon. Operation Aqubah was a series of air strikes in May along with artillery bombardment of the PFLOAG at Hawf in the PDRY in retaliation for the destruction of Habrut Fort on the border. Sarfait remained isolated because critical positions on the ridges that were to help provide a dominating position looking down on the coast could not be maintained due to lack of water and resupply.

Shortly after Operation Simba, a Jordanian delegation headed by a general visited the area, which resulted in King Hussain of Jordan sending 31 Hawker Hunter jets, twelve field guns and officers to the SAF. The Iranians also visited in August and a huge amount of military assistance was provided, including mortars, communications gear and posts for building fences. The help from abroad was most significant and only the start. This was perhaps the real success of Operation Simba.

THE BATTLE OF MIRBAT

Mirbat is a small coastal town 75km east of Salalah. In 1972 it was possibly the second largest town in Dhofar. SAF forces had had some important successes in 1972 and the PFLOAG wished to regain the initiative again by capturing a large town, killing the government's representative and local leaders, raise their flag, and then melt away into the mountains nearby after a day or two. In short, a brutal psychological strike within government held territory to undermine the people's faith in the Sultan and his forces was their aim. It was anticipated that it would result in a humiliation for the SAF and government and a subsequent drop in morale and a loss of faith by the local population. It would also cause the SAF to expend much time and energy searching for the enemy and the SAF would be obliged to put more resources into the town for its future protection.

It was known by the PFLOAG that the coastal town of Mirbat was lightly protected by a platoon of DG, and a small number of Askars, and that they were all lightly armed. It seemed a perfect target for them. Importantly the road to Salalah was easy for them to mine and ambush while making SAF reinforcement difficult.

The defensive positions in the town included several fortifications:
- The *Wali's* fort on the town's northwest. It was manned by a group of 30 Northern Oman Askars that were essentially used as gate keepers and for guard duties for the town *Wali*. They were armed only with .303 bolt action rifles.
- The DG (Dhofar Gendarmerie) fort, with a 25-pounder gun outside it in a gun pit, on the north east side of the town and overlooking the airstrip. The DG was a platoon of 25 men second-line infantry armed with self-loading rifles (SLR) and a single light machine gun. The 25-pounder gun was under the command of Walid bin Khamis Al Badri of the SOA. Further to this there was a nine man DG piquet was situated on Jebel Ali in two locations.
- The BATT House was situated between the two forts on the north of the town, but closer towards the town. There the

British Army Training Team of 9 SAS men of B Squadron resided in their own house. Apart from their SLR personal weapons they had an 81mm mortar, .5 Browning Machine Gun and a General Purpose Machine Gun (GPMG). The team was led by Capt Mike Kealy.

- The Firqat house was on the west side of the town with a DG *sanger* (a small fortified outpost) to its north. When not on patrol the unit was about 60 strong, but the PFLOAG had enticed the Firqat based in Mirbat to investigate a planned incident inland, leaving only a dozen or so men to defend their accommodation albeit with captured modern communist assault rifles, a machine gun and a 2-inch mortar. The leader of Firqat Salah al-Din (FSD) was Muhammad Saíd al-Amri.

The enemy had a strength of between 200 and 250 men, and the commander of this force was a member of the PFLOAG Military Committee High Command, and his second in command was the commander of the Central Sector Unit. PFLOAG forces were armed with modern AK-47 assault rifles and had two 75mm RCLs, two 3-inch mortars, three 2-inch mortars, a Carl Gustaf rocket launcher, two Shpagin DShK heavy machine guns, one or two Goryunov medium machine guns, fifteen RPD light machine guns, four Degtyarev light machine guns and at least two and possibly as many as five RPG-2s (man portable, hand-held, antitank grenade launchers fired from the shoulder). Although the latter was primarily an anti-tank weapon it was also capable of destroying fortifications. This was to be the largest attack ever made against Omani forces during the entire war.

The Battle of Mirbat took place on 19 July 1972. The main enemy force gathered at Wadi Ghazir over 17 and 18 July and moved against Mirbat overnight on the 18th and 19th where they formed up into four half-company sized units. Two were tasked as assault groups and the other two acted as a reserve and a heavy weapons unit. Due to bad weather overnight, including a thunderstorm, and unfamiliar territory for some to negotiate, forming up for the attack was a delayed. At about five o'clock in the morning the enemy forces attacked a four-man piquet of DG deployed on Jebel Ali which overlooked the town. There were in fact two piquets on the Jebel, both tasked with providing advance warning of any impending attack. The first piquet's occupants were killed by the attackers but the other piquet of five men, who were close by, managed to escape and raise the alarm in the town and then moved to a defensive position close to the beach.

Surprise, a key element of the attack, was lost. The DG fort was attacked by a company-sized unit from the north east while the others split into ten-man sections as they formed a crescent around the town, making escape impossible for the defenders. Those in the DG fort fired back and their 25-pounder gun was fired over open sights at the perimeter wire where many of the enemy were located.

SAS Trooper Labalaba was helping Walid bin Khamis Al Badri (OA) at the gun pit but was wounded and radioed his fellow Fijian Trooper Savesaki for assistance. Savesaki ran under heavy fire to the gun pit to assist. Concurrently, the BATT House defenders opened fire with all weapons. Realizing that the gun was crucial to combating the swarming enemy at the perimeter fence Captain Kealy SAS sprinted to the gun pit with medical orderly Trooper Tobin. There they found Savesaki badly wounded and the gunner Walid bin Khamis Al Badri was also hurt. There was no assistance from the fort as they were restrained by heavy incoming fire and Trooper Labalaba was shot dead. The enemy made a concerted effort to capture the gun, but fortuitously SOAF Strikemaster jets arrived in time and caught the enemy in the open, thus stopping the attack

on the gun pit. While this was happening the town's Firqah saw the enemy trying to cut off the town from the south at the beach. Leaving four men with the machine gun and mortar in the Firqah House, the leader of the group took the remaining men through the town to confront the enemy. They cleared the insurgents from the coast, killing some and capturing four but their leader was wounded in the process.

Both the Dhofar Gendarmerie and SAS had radioed Salalah for assistance. Once daylight came up, the SOAF was able to send a helicopter to Mirbat to see what was happening and advised Salalah that heavy fighting was taking place. With the lifting of the fog the Strikemaster fighter/bombers were able to come in and fly at very low levels and strafed any enemy in the open. One of the three Strikemaster's was hit by a heavy machine gun round and had to limp back to base with a hole in its' wing. Another aircraft had 12 bullet holes in it, but that did not affect its mission. A SOAF helicopter tried to evacuate the wounded but was driven off by heavy fire. Corporal Roger Chapman SAS was able to radio instructions to a Strikemaster for target acquisition of selected targets.

Meanwhile in Salalah, G Squadron SAS had arrived 24 hours earlier in a planned move to relieve B Squadron in the province and was fully equipped to go to the firing range to zero-in their weapons. Being fully armed they were very quickly able to dispatch 23 fully prepared officers and men to Mirbat in three helicopters to drive the already severely mauled Adoo back off to the fastness of the mountains. They arrived at 9.15 am, while the SOAF made another air to ground strike against the enemy. The SAS Troop from G Squadron clambered out of their helicopters and split into two ten-man sections and a command detachment before heading off into the town. After this, the first helicopter successfully landed at the BATT House and the wounded were taken on board, it then moved to the Dhofar Gendarmerie Fort and picked up the other wounded. A second Troop of G Squadron was landed at 10.20 am and included medical orderlies. Small pockets of enemy were quickly rooted out to the south and another helicopter arrived with a platoon of Northern Frontier Regiment (NFR). The SAS and NFR joined together and moved up to the BATT House. The SOAF attacked gun sites on Jebel Ali and the NFR moved in and occupied the area. G Squadron forced a number of enemy to retreat north via the beach where they were stopped by the returning FSD Firqah, killing nine enemy in the contact. At 10.30 Tobin, Savesaki and Walid bin Khamis al-Badri were flown off to Salalah for medical treatment. Salalah sent a half-company of B Company NFR to Mirbat where they enfiladed the enemy's flanks. By lunch time the battle was won.

The casualties of the Adoo are difficult to ascertain as several sources provide widely differing numbers of dead and injured, but what is known is that up to 86 enemy soldiers were either killed, captured or severely wounded. The defending forces had only a small number killed or wounded. Mirbat was a major defeat for the PFLOAG and an important action because many of the best troops that PFLOAG had were either killed or disabled. Never again did they attempt to attack the sultan's forces in large numbers. After the dust had settled and peace was declared a few years later, military historians, experts and strategists recognised that the battle of Mirbat was a decisive turning point. While there were many important actions, both military and civil, that contributed to the final successful outcome of the war, Mirbat was without a doubt a very important victory within the overall campaign. The PFLOAG had invested an overwhelming force, including many of their best and highly trained soldiers that had studied and trained

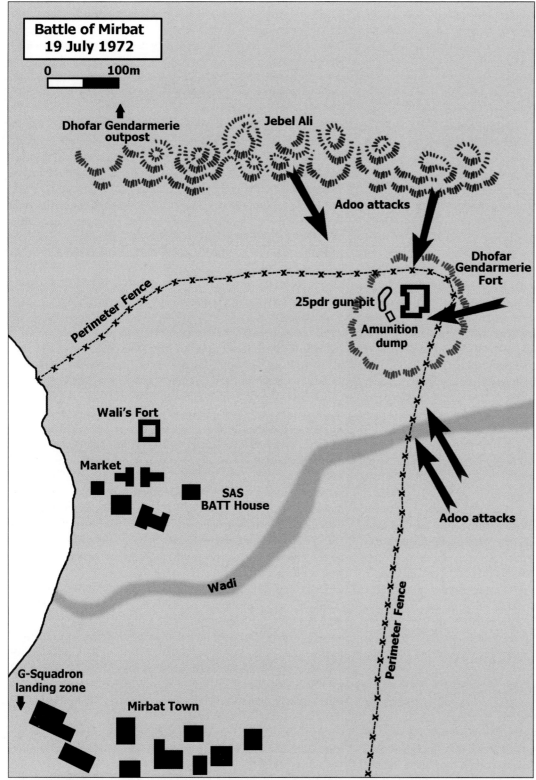

Battle of Mirbat
19 July 1972

0   100m

Dhofar Gendarmerie
outpost

Jebel Ali

Adoo attacks

Perimeter Fence

Dhofar
Gendarmerie
Fort

25pdr gun pit

Amunition
dump

Wali's Fort

Market

SAS
BATT House

Wadi

Adoo attacks

Perimeter Fence

G-Squadron
landing zone

Mirbat Town

A map of Mirbat and the battle of 19 July 1972. (Map by Tom Cooper)

Surrendered Enemy Personnel to SAF forces. The utter defeat of the enemy by a staggeringly small defending group was a major psychological blow and they lost credibility with the warrior-class men on the Jebel.

THE SAF GRADUALLY GETS THE UPPER HAND

When the SAF pursued the defensive line policy it did not have enough resources and troops to ensure the fortified lines system would succeed. It was then that Oman asked for regional support. The Shah of Iran, Mohammad Reza Pahlavi, was concerned about creeping communism within the Gulf region and made the decision to provide military assistance to his friend the Sultan of Oman and, in return, provide his forces with combat experience. In November 1972, the first 340 Iranian ground troops arrived in Oman to help set up bases for a brigade of the Imperial Iranian Army Aviation (IIAA), equipped with 32 AB.205 and Bell 206 JetRanger helicopters. Eventually, the number of Iranian troops deployed in the country grew to more than 3,200 – most of whom were assigned to one expeditionary brigade: operating in close coordination with the SAF, they gradually subdued the insurgents in the mountains, before launching their first offensive operations.

Many other operations took place in 1972 including Operation Hornbeam. Troops moved onto the Jebel as a precursor to creating a permanent Hornbeam Line to foil resupply to insurgents

in communist military battle camps and military schools. Their top leaders and foreign advisers had planned the attack meticulously, even down to the fact that they did not expect the SOAF to be able to respond due to low fog coverage at the time of the planned attack. Failure by the PFLOAG to take the supposed soft target of Mirbat was quite unexpected and they never fully recovered from the loss of hard-core trained fighting men and were never able to deploy large concentrated forces to attack objectives again. Younger fighters lost faith in their commanders. The hierarchy took their anger out on those they thought had failed them by judging them and executing them. This entire episode combined to cause a noticeable increase of

through to the eastern and central areas of Dhofar, with work starting on the Line in December 1973 and finished in June 1974. During December 1972 Operation Jason commenced in northern Oman. This successful operation was the result of information provided from a surrendered Dhofari who was sent to Muscat to watch for PFLOAG members in the streets and markets, where he saw Muhammad Talib, a member of the Front's Executive Committee, and reported this to the authorities. Talib was quickly taken into custody and divulged his knowledge of the activities of the Front. Consequently, many arrests were made, new information became available about their network and almost 80 PFLOAG terrorists were captured, which was fortuitous as the PFLOAG had planned to open a second front in the north and had a huge stash of arms and ammunition hidden away.

On 18 January 1973, the Imperial Iranian Air Force (IIAF) also deployed four McDonnell Douglas F-4D Phantom II fighter-bombers at Bait al Falaj AB. Four additional F-4Ds were deployed to Masirah AB. Supported by two C-130 transports that were hauling ground crews, spares and weapons, this temporary detachment was to last for five years, in the course of which the F-4Ds were replaced by more advanced F-4Es, which carried an internally installed 20mm cannon.

Concurrent with fighting a difficult war where not all in the Dhofar were the Sultans men, a major policy rethink of the war took place in 1973. The commander of the SAF recognised that the Dhofar War required a more holistic perspective to combat the enemy. It was realized that a better balance of military forces along with a smarter political understanding and a desire to help the people of Dhofar was required. A "hearts and minds" campaign was implemented to show that the Sultan and his government wanted to help the population by providing medical help, improving their lives with building projects and drilling for water and providing schools. SAF engineers would continue their military duties but also be available for civil development. From a military perspective the establishment of Firqats in the SAF for irregular warfare by using turned Surrendered Enemy Personnel and the local Dhofar mountain population added a new dimension to the gathering of intelligence and the isolation and destruction of enemy infiltrated forces. GPMGs and 81mm mortars, along with air portable guns, were introduced across the army and more infantry battalions were raised. Furthermore, the practice of having mixed Arab and Baluch units ceased.

A Soviet-made PDRY Air Force Il-28 Beagle bomber dropped a stick of eight bombs on Makinat Shihan, a well about 56 kilometres north-west of Habrut, on 18 November 1973, in the only recorded incident of its kind. The area at that time was invested by D Squadron of the Oman Gendarmerie, a mortar section and assault pioneer platoon of the Jebel Regiment plus a troop of the Armoured Car Squadron. The military were attempting to repair the well for civilian use. No casualties were recorded and the attack may have been a response to previous incursions into the PDRY.

During December 1973, mainly Iranian forces re-opened the Salalah – Midway road.

Modern jet fighters, transport aircraft and more helicopters arrived from Iran in 1974 and the Imperial Iranian Navy scoured the coast to ensure the enemy were unable to supply their forces by sea. A defensive military line known as the Hornbeam Line was built and completed by mid-1974, which had major assistance from Jordanian Combat Engineers and Iranian Special Forces. The line was about 60 kilometres in length extending from the sea, through the mountains to the desert. Camel caravan transport for the insurgents was no longer possible and everything had to be carried by the men. A second defensive line was built by the Iranians in 1974, which was sited further west towards the border with PDRY and known as the Damavand Line. The Civil Action Teams (or CAT) and Civil Aid Department (or CAD) were important groups whose tasks could be started once the SAF had taken over control of various areas formerly under enemy control. Certain factors on the Jebel were catalysts for the pacification of the Eastern Sector once the SAF had defeated the Adoo in the field. These included the building of the Hornbeam Line which helped to interdict the Adoo as they tried to infiltrate into the Eastern Sector with men, arms

and supplies, and the opening of the road from Salalah to Midway (Thumrait), had made civil development more possible. Once an area was taken by the SAF, water was drilled for, and shelter for the CAT was made. The CATs worked on the Eastern Jebel from 1974.

The insurgents received their first shipment of Soviet-made Strela-2 man-portable air defence systems (MANPADS, better known in the west for their NATO-designation 'SA-7 Grail') in 1975. The SA-7s saw their first action in August of the same year, when they were used to shoot down one of two Strikemaster's scrambled from Salalah for an attack on the Sherishitti Caves. Fortunately, the pilot ejected safely into the Wadi Jawt, and was subsequently recovered by an AB.205 helicopter that was heading to Sarfait with a load of troops and supplies. The second missile missed the other Strikemaster, while a third narrowly missed the helicopter. The appearance of SA-7s forced the SOAF to change its tactics and apply modifications. Henceforth, all the AB.205s received tunnels over their exhausts, which dispersed the engine heat directly into the rotor downwash. The helicopter and Strikemaster pilots also trained to operate at higher altitudes and descend only while flying in tight spirals, thus making tracking with SA-7s more difficult for the enemy. Nevertheless, another Strikemaster was hit in September by an improved SA-7B, which had a higher engagement envelope. The pilot succeeded in bringing back his badly damaged aircraft to Manston airfield. At least seven SA-7s were fired at SOAF aircraft on 31 October shooting down one AB-205 helicopter. Twenty-three SA-7s are believed to have been fired within a 12-month period, but only three scored hits.

From July 1974 the PFLOAG became known as the Popular Front for the Liberation of Oman (PFLO). Also in 1974, the Imperial Iranian Task Force was reinforced from battalion strength to a brigade and this brigade was sent to Aydim (Manston) in November. In December, two battalions of Iranian forces – each reinforced through the addition of one firqah – launched Operation Nadir with the intention of capturing the Sherishitti Caves and Rakhyut on the coast. The Iranians suffered heavy casualties and proved reluctant to press home their attack, and so the plan was changed. They were then tasked to take a position known as Everest and capture Rakhyut. Meanwhile the Jebel Regiment was deployed to menace the Sherishitti Caves area. A mixed force of about 600 SAF troops were assembled at Manston airfield and a number of assaults were launched against enemy forces in the caves area, but with little success and with casualties on both sides. However, there were some positive outcomes; tracks were made for armoured cars and vehicles; enemy supply routes were interdicted and new bases dug in; and Iranian forces consolidated their positions to the east into the Damavand Line from Craterfield, Araqi, and Everest to Rakhyut. This fortified line consisted of mines and barbed wire and was a serious deterrent to the insurgents.

The Civil Aid Department (CAD) was established in January 1975 to coordinate management of the projects and they worked in concert with the armed forces. The building of infrastructure for the villages, such as schools, mosques, roads and clinics gave good reason for the local population to support the Sultan as the godless Adoo only brought death and destruction. Another significant development was on the diplomatic front, where Omani and British diplomatic efforts brought about better relations between Oman and Saudi Arabia and consequently the Arab League, and eventually the United Nations. Because of this, the PFLOAG was no longer seen as a legitimate anti-British or anti-colonial resistance force. Jordan, Abu Dhabi and Saudi Arabia all sent various forms of military assistance to Oman. Jordan not only supplied 31 Hawker

Hunter fighter-bombers, artillery and engineers, but a battalion of special forces of over 500 men. Iran increased its military assistance with more men and naval and air assets. With Oman's success the PFLOAG started to become diplomatically isolated.

Operation Dharb occurred over 4 and 5 January 1975 and was mounted to assist the Iranian advance on Rakhuyt which they captured on 6 January 1975. On 21 February, Operation Himaar commenced with attacking the enemy 9th June Regiment at Wadi Ashwaq and in the Hornbeam Line area, capturing and destroying large amounts of ammunition and weapons including light weapons, mortars, RCL and a Katyusha rocket launcher. The Jordanian 91st Special Forces Battalion took responsibility to guard the Midway Road for six months from March.

Operation Kuhuf (Caves) was launched in October as a diversion for the later Operation Hadaf, the plan being to make the PFLO believe that the SAF would simultaneously be attacking Sherishitti and the supply routes between Sarfait and the sea. Also in October, the Iranians carried out Operation Sa'id on the 17th, which was a further diversion for Operation Hadaf. Two reasons for the operation were to draw off Front troops from other areas and, importantly, the position was a threat to the Sherishitti Caves where the Front had a major storage area. The Iranian troops were landed by helicopter on the Shirawz ridge west of the Damavand Line. In concert with the deployment of the troops there was a massive ship to shore bombardment by three Iranian warships to cover their arrival and SAF artillery also supported the operation. The Iranians still came under heavy fire however and had twelve men killed and four wounded.

Operation Hadaf was planned to clear the territory around the Sherishitti Caves, Zakhir, and Sha'bawt while the enemy expected a full-scale attack on the caves. Once the area had been cleared of enemy personnel the Frontier Force went back and captured the Sherishitti Caves themselves; over 100 tons of weapons, ammunition and stores was found there. Operation Hadaf was concluded by 18 November and with its success Operation Hilwah was launched on November 28 by the Frontier Force and captured Dalkhuyt on 1 December. The following day, the Darra Ridge was cleared by the Frontier Force, from where they were able to join with the Muscat Regiment advancing from Sarfait. This is considered to be the end of organized resistance in Dhofar, but sporadic fighting did continue.

On 11 December 1975 HM Sultan Qaboos stated that the war

was officially over. The insurgent's 9th June Regiment was crippled and lost its supplies, though about a half-company remained in the Bait Handawb. Gradually the insurgent numbers dwindled away and they were recalled to the PDRY. The insurgency had failed.

The Sultanate of Oman declared a ceasefire along the border with the PDRY on 10 March 1976, but occasional incidents continued in the Eastern Area through to September of that year and minor incidents and fatalities occurred until March 1980.

A major border incident occurred in 1987 on the PDYR border. There were a number of skirmishes with troops from the PDYR in Toyota pickup trucks armed with DShK 12.7mm heavy machine guns and casualties were inflicted upon the lightly armed Omani forces. A motorised infantry force was sent by the PDRY to the border but it was destroyed by SEPECAT Jaguar fighter bombers of the Sultanate of Oman Air Force (SOAF). There were no further incidents, and peace talks ensued.

CONCLUSION OF THE DHOFAR WAR

Many factors contributed to the successful outcome of the war in Dhofar. The strategy of building defensive lines across western Dhofar was the principal one. It was initiated with the Leopard Line, which was a series of piquets from Mughsayl on the coast to the Negd. Renamed the Hornbeam Line, this was later modified to become a barbed wire fence line with associated minefields and obstacles, reaching 53 kilometres north of the coast. Its further extension known as the Hammer Line was built from Midway Road to the Hornbeam Line. Combined, the lines prevented camel caravan trains loaded with arms and ammunition from moving freely all over Dhofar. While they did not stop all enemy soldiers getting through, they did restrict them, and those that made it through could only take supplies that they could carry themselves. The last line to be built was further west. This was made by the Iranians: the Damavand Line, named after the highest mountain in Iran. While a great success, as was the Iranian assistance and provision of troops, aircraft, and helicopters, this military intervention came at a heavy price in lives for the inexperienced Iranian military. Iran had 14,682 military personnel rotated in and out of the country and suffered the loss of 719 killed and 1,404 wounded in action. Other factors included British military expertise and leadership and a relatively small number of British Army SAS, RE, RA, Medical personnel and others, plus RAF pilots and ground crew as well as units of the RAF Regiment at Salalah; some estimates indicate that there were never more than 1,000 military personnel in total. Other factors include diplomatic and political expertise, air superiority, control of the seas, winning hearts and minds, military and economic assistance from Iran in particular, but also from Jordan, Abu Dhabi and Saudi Arabia, clever strategy and the ability to turn many of the enemy to fight against their former comrades. The success of the Dhofar War not only united the people behind Sultan Qaboos, but enabled him to invest the oil-revenue,

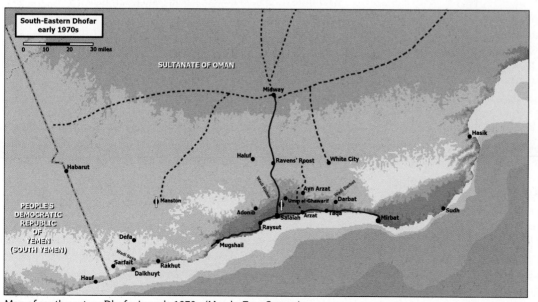

Map of south-eastern Dhofar in early 1970s. (Map by Tom Cooper)

Sayyid Shihab bin Faysal inspecting SAF Troops at Bait al Falaj, in October 1960. From left to right: Captain Aziz MR, Captain Muhammad Jalal MR, Pat Waterfield (who served as Military Secretary at the time), and David Smiley. (Malcolm G. Dennison via J. E. Peterson)

Sayyid Shihab bin Faysal pinning a medal on an unknown soldier at Bait al Falaj, ca 1958-1960. R. David Smiley (left) and Richard Anderson are watching. (Malcolm G Dennison via J. E. Peterson)

PFLO pin badge for the Popular Front for the Liberation of Oman. From July 1974 the Popular Front for the Liberation of Oman and Arab Gulf (PFLOAG) became known as the Popular Front for the Liberation of Oman (PFLO). The badge has a white background with red letters on the outer circle and the centre has black outlines with a red AK 47 in the centre. (Courtesy: The Badge Collectors Circle)

which had only started to come on-line from 1967, in his people and his country. Iran and the Arab Middle East saw the threat of communism evaporate and also assured of the continuance of the

transport of oil through the Straits of Hormuz. For the British the Dhofar campaign was certainly one of the most successful counterinsurgency campaigns of the twentieth century.

Due to Oman's regional support, Egypt cut its support for the PFLOAG and belatedly chose to foster better relations with the Gulf States. China sought better relations with Iran and ended its support for the PFLOAG, as did Iraq after the Algiers Agreement with Iran in 1975.

POST DHOFAR WAR

With the successful conclusion of the Dhofar War, the SAF moved gradually away from its traditional role of acting as an armed internal police force and fighting counter insurgency wars. Sultan Qaboos – with his enlightened views and passion for bringing his country into the modern world with health and prosperity for his people – and the new-found oil wealth provided the stability the country needed. Governmental and civil agencies gradually replaced the military in providing roads, drilling for water, basic health care, education and the other requirements for a successful state. The Royal Oman Police also became a successful and professional force. Since the end of the Dhofar campaign the SAF moved forward to become a modern, well equipped, trained and competent force that was able to defend the state against external aggression. This change of role began from about 1980 and included many new weapon systems. Battle tanks were obtained, the artillery expanded to two regiments and reequipped with new 105 mm Light Guns, and two medium batteries of 130 mm guns. Air defence was provided by Blowpipe SAM's. Motorization of the infantry took place in 1982 with Pinzgauer high-mobility all-terrain vehicles. The other services and units all expanded throughout the 1980s. A battalion group with an artillery battery joined the Coalition Forces in 1990 against the Iraqi invasion of Kuwait. The RAO purchased MOWAG Piranha Armoured Fighting Vehicles in 1995 to equip the Desert Regiment. By the end of the decade the armoured units had reached brigade size with the purchase of more tanks including Scorpions, Challenger 2 and M60A3s. Self-propelled 155mm G6 guns were ordered from South Africa to replace the older 130mm guns. A fourth artillery regiment was raised for air defence. Interestingly, the engineers formed an Armoured Engineer Squadron with Nuclear Biological and Chemical defence capabilities. At the beginning of the 21st century the Air, Naval and Land components had all modernised for their new role in the defence of Oman and the GCC States. The RAO had become a divisional-sized army comprising two infantry brigades and an armoured brigade. Further to this the division had support from an artillery brigade and all of the engineer, signal, and supporting services required. Another infantry regiment, the Muscat Regiment, became mechanized with the purchase of more Piranha armoured fighting vehicles in 2003. That same year saw RAO deploy operationally with the Peninsula Shield Force for the defence of Kuwait. New thinking in defence brought in the Border Guard Brigade in 2008, which was fully equipped by 2011. Major joint exercises were conducted with the United Kingdom and the GCC in Oman in 2001 and 2007 respectively. Signals and engineers also gained another regiment each that decade.

THE GULF COOPERATION COUNCIL (GCC), THE PENINSULA SHIELD FORCE (PSF), THE GULF WAR, AND THE IRAQ WAR

The Gulf Cooperation Council is a regional intergovernmental political and economic union which comprises Kuwait, Bahrain, Qatar, United Arab Emirates, Oman, and Saudi Arabia. The Charter of the Gulf Cooperation Council was signed on 25 May

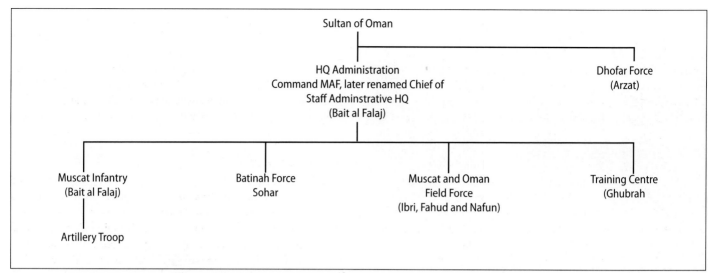

Structure of the Muscat Armed Forces and Dhofar Force, 1955

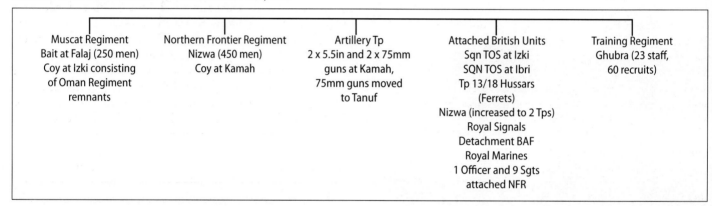

SAF Deployment and Formation as of April 1958

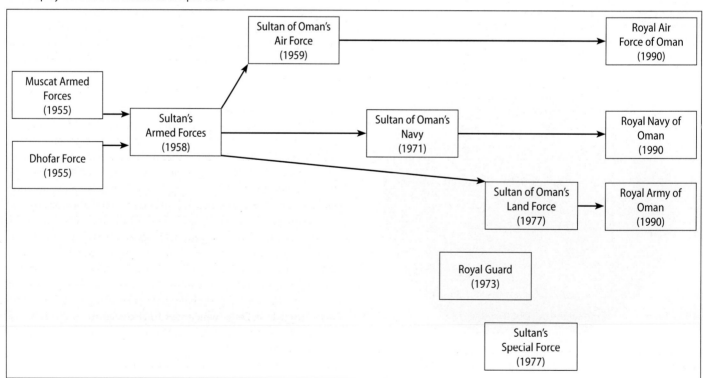

Development of the Armed Forces of Oman, 1955-1990. Note the D.F. was integrated into the S.A.F. in 1970.

1981, which formally established the institution. A decision was made in 1984 by the GCC to create a joint military force of 10,000 soldiers sub-divided into two brigades and known as The Peninsula Shield Force. As the military wing of the (GCC) its purpose is to deter and respond to military aggression against any of the GCC member countries. Based in Saudi Arabia, close to the Kuwaiti and Iraqi borders, it consists of combat and combat support assets from each of the GCC countries. In August 1990, Iraq invaded GCC member Kuwait, and Oman provided the Oman Coast Regiment to bolster the defences of Saudi Arabia. This unit was then replaced by the Northern Frontier Regiment Battalion Group (NFRBG), an artillery battery and a Milan anti-tank guided missile troop to serve in Saudi Arabia with coalition partners as part of the GCC contribution to the land war for the liberation of Kuwait. Omani forces acted as a sub-unit of a Saudi Arabian Brigade and were deployed into Kuwait on the second day of the ground offensive on 25 February 1991 and participated in the liberation of Kuwait City. There were no casualties incurred by the NFRBG. Furthermore, Oman became a base area and staging post for the United States Air Force and the British Royal Air Force which deployed to the Arabian Gulf. During that war the Masirah AB was used by transport and refuelling aircraft. The RAFO (Royal Air Force of Oman) did not participate in air strikes on Iraq.

In February 2003, 10,000 PSF Troops and two naval vessels were deployed to Kuwait during the Iraq War to assist and defend Kuwait from possible Iraqi aggression but did not participate in operations against the Iraqi forces. The Desert Regiment, now equipped with Piranha armoured cars, was deployed as a part of the GCC Peninsula Shield Force in the defence of Kuwait. Support Troop from the Sultan's Oman Para provided anti-tank weapons with their Panhard armoured cars. During 2011, the PSF was called into service to assist Bahrain during the Bahraini uprising by providing temporary border security and protection of vital and strategic areas while Bahraini forces focused on internal security.

Table 1: Rulers of Muscat and Oman in the 20th Century

Period	Name
1888-1913	Faisal bin Turki
1913-1932	Taimur bin Faisal
1932-1970	Said III bin Taimur
	Sultan of Oman
1970-	Qaboos bin Said

Table 2: Imams of Oman since 1913

Period	Name
1913-1920	Salim bin Rashid al-Kharusi
1920-1954	Mohammed bin Abdullah al Khalili
1954-1959	Ghalib bin Ali bin Hilal al Hinai

Table 3: Military Commanders of the Sultanate of Muscat and Oman and the Sultanate of Oman

Period	Name	Official Title
1955-1958	Colonel P. R. M. Waterfield	Administrative Commandant Muscat Armed Forces
1958-1976	Colonel P. R. M. Waterfield	Chief of Staff (1958-1976)
1958-1976	Brigadier C. C. Maxwell	Deputy Commander Sultan's Armed Forces
1976-1981	Brigadier P. T. Thwaites	Chairman of the Joint Staff
1981-	Brigadier Hasan bin Ihasan bin Nasib	Chairman of the Joint Staff

1981-1984	General Sir Timorthy Creasey	Chief of the Defence Staff
1984-1987	Lieutenant-General J. P. B. C. Watts	Chief of the Defence Staff
1987-1990	Lieutenant-General Hamid bin Said al-Awfi	Chief of Staff, Sultan's Armed Forces
1990-2003	Lieutenant-General Khamis bin Hamayd al-Kalbani	Chief of Staff, Sultan's Armed Forces
2003-	Lieutenant-General Ahmad bin Harith al-Nabhani	

Table 4: Commanders, Sultan's Armed Forces, 1958-1977

Period	Name
1958-1961	Colonel D. De C. Smiley
1961-1964	Colonel H. R. D. Oldman
1964-1967	Colonel A. D. Lewis
1967-1970	Brigadier C. W. B. Purlon
1970-1972	Brigadier J. D. C. Graham
1972-1975	Major-General T. M. Creasey
1975-1977	Major-General K. Perkins

Table 5: Commanders, Sultan of Oman's Land Forces, 1977-1990

Period	Name
1977-1979	Major-General The O'Morchoe
1979-1984	Major-General J. P. B. C. Watts
1984-1987	Major-General Nasib bin Hamad al-Ruwayhi
1987-1990	Major-General Khamis bin Humayd al-Kalbani

Table 6: Commanders, Royal Army of Oman, 1990-today

Period	Name
1990-2000	Major-General Ali bin Rashid al-Kalbani
2000-2003	Major-General Ahmad bin Harith al-Nabhani
2003-2013	Major-General Sa'id bin Nasir bin Sulayman bin al-Salmi
2013-	Liwa Rukn Matar bin Salim bin Rashid al-Balushi

Table 7: Commanders, Sultan of Oman's Air Force, 1959-1990

Period	Name
1959-1962	Squadron Leader G. B. Atkinson
1962-1964	Wing Commander J. A. Horrell
1964-1967	Wing Commander B. Enthwistle
1967-1970	Squadron Leader A. G. Bridges

Table 8: Commanders, Royal Air Force of Oman, 1990-today

Period	Name
1990-2002	Air Vice Marshal Talib bin Miran al-Ra'isi
1992-2003	Air Vice Marshal Muhammad bin Mahfuz bin Said al-Aridi
2003-2012	Air Vice Marshal Yahya bin Rashid al-Jumáh
2012-	Air Vice Marshal Matar bin Ali al-Obaidani

Table 9: Commanders, Sultan of Oman's Navy, 1971-1990

Period	Name
1971-1973	Commander D. R. Williams
1973-1976	Captain R. P. Brooke-Popham
1976-1980	Commodore H. Mucklow
1980-1985	Rear Admiral J. P. Gunning
1985-1990	Rear Admiral H. M. Balfour

Table 10: Commanders, Royal Navy of Oman, 1990-today

Period Name	
1990-2004	Rear Admiral Sayyid Shihab bin Tariq al Said
2004-2008	Rear Admiral Salim bin Abdullah bin Rashid al-Alawi
2008-	Rear Admiral Abdullah bin Khamis al-Rashed

2
SULTAN'S ARMED FORCES

OMAN'S MILITARY COMMAND COSSAF

The Chief of Staff Sultan's Armed Forces (COSSAF) position was established in 1987, replacing the Chief of Defence Staff. COSSAF consists of a headquarters and coordinates the three services, the Royal Army of Oman (RAO), Royal Air Force of Oman (RAFO) and Royal Navy of Oman (RNO) but has no operational command over them. A Joint HQ has not been established at the time of writing and the RAO, RAFO and RNO are virtually autonomous services operationally, but liaise closely. Their commanders have direct access to His Majesty in his role as Minister of Defence. COSSAF reports to the separate office of the Minister for Defence Affairs. The Office of COSSAF consists of several directorates including: Military Welfare Services, Moral Guidance, SAF Museum, International Shooting Unit, Command and Staff College, and Information Technology Services. The Royal Guard of Oman (RGO) and Sultan's Special Forces (SSF) are totally separate entities and come under command of the Royal Office though in large scale army exercises they often send troops to participate with the RAO. SSF works closely with RAFO and RNO on anti-piracy and anti-hijacking operations/exercises.

SULTAN'S ARMED FORCES
11 INFANTRY BRIGADE

Dhofar Area HQ was formed in 1971 and was located at Umm al Gwariff Camp. Re-designation to Dhofar Brigade occurred in 1972 reflecting the increased numbers of troops. A further name change took place in 1976 when it became Southern Oman Brigade, which

also had command of Firqat Forces. It also had control over naval and air assets within its area of operation. With continual expansion the brigade was again renamed on 23 July 1991 as 11 Infantry Brigade. The number 11 symbolises 11 December 1975, the day the Dhofar War was declared over.

23 INFANTRY BRIGADE

HQ Northern Oman Command was stood up in 1973 at MAM and the Northern Oman Headquarters was responsible for the various units that were deployed in the north of the country. On 21 September 1976 it was re-designated as HQ Northern Oman Brigade though duties and size remained unchanged. From 1980 a large expansion occurred with new units being integrated into the brigade. On 23 July 1991 the brigade was re-designated 23 Infantry Brigade. The number 23 symbolises the day Sultan Qaboos replaced his father on 23 July 1970.

BORDER GUARD BRIGADE (BGB)

In 2007 it was recognised that there was a requirement for a military unit to control the border with Saudi Arabia from northern Dhofar to the Dhahira Region. Consequently, three regiments of border guards were formed, creating a new Border Guard Brigade. The first regiment was raised in 2008 at Ibri, and the second regiment followed in mid-2009 at Mazyona in Dhofar. The Brigade HQ was raised later in 2009 and was first based in Shaafa but moved to Haima in 2011. A third regiment was raised in 2011 based at Haima, and a fourth was being raised in 2018.

UNIFORM AND REGALIA

The Border Guard Brigade regiments all wear a yellow beret with the standard RAO Badge. The officers' wire badge is woven on black felt. The three regiments wear a unique square patch behind their beret badge to denote which battalion they are from. Each regiment has its own lanyard, stable belt and regimental arm flash. Traditional colours are as listed in Table 11.

Table 11: Regalia of the Border Guard Brigade

Element	Beret Patch	Lanyard	Stable Belt
Brigade HQ	none	yellow with brown	yellow over brown with gold buckle and RAO device
1 Regiment	yellow	yellow	brown over yellow with gold buckle and RAO device
2 Regiment	green	yellow with red and green	green over yellow with gold buckle and RAO device
3 Regiment	red	yellow with red stripe winding around	red over yellow with gold buckle and RAO device

HQ MUSANDAM SECTOR (HQ MS)

HQ MS traces its ancestry back to the Oman Gendarmerie Peninsular Sector (PENSEC), which was located at Khasab from 1971. PENSEC Squadron remained at Khasab until it became a company of the Oman Coast Regiment in 1978. By June that year the squadron was replaced by the Peninsular Reinforcement Battalion (PRB) which provided a company for Musandam and rotated with other battalions. During late 1980 the Musandam Security Force was raised and joined the PRB Company in the sector. The administration by the Khasab Station Staff Office, which had been opened in 1977, was found to be inadequate for the expanded military presence. Consequently, in 1981, HQ PENSEC was built and opened at Khasab and came under the command of HQ Northern Oman. HQ NOM was later re-designated 23 Infantry Brigade. HQ PENSEC was renamed HQ Musandam Sector later in the 1980s but retained its control of military affairs. A decision was made to place the HQ directly under the command of HQ RAO in 2003.

MUDARRAAT SULTAN OMAN (MSO)
Armoured Car Troop, Armoured Car Squadron, Armoured Force of Oman, Oman Tank Force, Sultan of Oman's Armoured Regiment & Mudarraat Sultan Oman

The MSO was established when the Dhofar Force was absorbed into the SAF in 1970. At that time the unit had four Ferret scout cars and 3 Cadillac Gage V-100 Commando carriers, located at Arzat – which was also the HQ of the Dhofar Gendarmerie – where their role was to patrol the Salalah Plain. The troop became part of the Armoured Car Squadron a few months later.

The Armoured Car Squadron was raised in March 1971, and later that month was enlarged through the addition of eight Saladin and four Ferret armoured cars. Following their arrival at Bait al Falaj, training of the new squadron proceeded at Bid Bid. The former Dhofar Force Troop remained at Arzat in support. A soldier defected with a V-100 Commando which was found destroyed in the Wadi Arzat and another Commando was destroyed by an RPG-7 when ambushed. The last remaining Commando suffered from lack of spares and was eventually removed from the order of battle. The four remaining Ferret scout cars were renamed RECCE Troop. 21 February 1971 saw the troop's first firefight in a successful clash with 25 of the enemy's forces. Operation Beaufort took place on the Jebel over 10-11 March, in conjunction with the Muscat Regiment, a company of Northern Frontier Regiment and the Armoured Car Squadron at the Wadi Darbat. The new troops were moved to Midway on 17 September 1971. The contemporary

British Unipower tank transporter carrying the Omani variant of the Challenger 2 Main Battle Tank, which has additional air conditioning and extra cooling systems that are necessary for the MBT to operate in more extreme desert conditions. Some of the "desertisation" modifications include the 'Skirt Plate' which involved the incorporation of new seals, dust strips and track guard. (Courtesy: Muqaddam Ian Buttenshaw)

Challenger 2 MBT of Type 38 Regiment, with two squadrons of 19 tanks. (Courtesy: Muqaddam Ian Buttenshaw)

composition of the MSO is listed in Table 12.

Table 12: Mudarraat Sultan Oman Armoured Car Squadron, 1971

Element	Equipment	Notes
HQ	2 Saladin & 2 Ferret	
Support Troop	4 Saladin	
Recce Troop	4 Ferret	based in Arzat
Training Troop	2 Saladin & 2 Ferret	based in Bait al Falaj

In May 1973 the squadron received 12 Saladin armoured cars from the Abu Dhabi Defence Force. That same year an EME LAD

(Light Aid Detachment) was formed. By 1974 there were troops at Salalah, Thumrait, Makinat Shihan, Jibjat, and MAM. Six more Saladins were provided by Abu Dhabi and 18 new Saladins were received later in 1974. A Guided Weapons Troop equipped with TOW anti-tank missiles was created in 1975. By 1992, TOW were mounted on Land Cruisers in an Anti-Tank Squadron, which was transferred to SOP in 1994.

The Armoured Car Squadron was retitled Armoured Force of Oman during 1978, which consisted of two squadrons. One squadron was at MAM Camp in Northern Oman and the other was at Thumrait by 1980. A third squadron was stood up at MAM in 1980. American M60 tanks were purchased and in August 1980 became the Oman Tank Force located at Maabela. British Scorpion light tanks followed and the Sultan of Oman Armoured Regiment (SOAR) was formed in 1981. A move to Sultan bin Saif Camp in Shaafa took place in April 1986. The armoured forces expanded into several regiments. By 1982-1983, the Saladins were being phased out and replaced by Scorpion light tanks. Chieftain MBTs were introduced around the same time and thus the structure of the SOAR was re-organized as listed in Table 13.

Table 13: SOAR in 1982-1983

Element	Equipment	Notes
HQ Squadron		
A Squadron	Scorpion	
B Squadron	Scorpion	
C Squadron	Scorpion	
D Squadron	M60A1 & Chieftain	
E Squadron	Chieftain	training element

The regiment moved to Sultan bin Saif Camp in 1986/87 at Shaafa, when it was officially presented with its colours. Ever since, its officers and other ranks have worn a black beret, lanyard in black woven with two strands. More tanks were acquired in 1990 with a regiment of M60A3 tanks being formed, enabling an expansion into a brigade designated as the Mudarraat Sultan Oman (MSO) – or Sultan of Oman's Armour – in 1991. Four years later, this unit was organized as listed in Table 14:

Table 14: MSO in 1995

Element	Equipment	Notes
HQ Squadron		
1 MBT Regiment	M60A3	entirely re-equipped with Challenger 2 MBTs in 2000
2 MBT Regiment	M60A3	
Armoured Reconnaissance Regiment	Scorpion	

SULTAN OF OMAN ARTILLERY (SOA)

The Muscat Levy Corps received artillery in the late 1920s consisting of two 2.75-inch BL screw guns from India. These guns remained in service until 1957 – when they were last fired in anger during Talib's rout of the Oman Regiment near Nizwa – and ammunition unavailability ensured the guns' demise. In 1942 a bone fide Artillery Troop was formed at Bait al Falaj within the Muscat Infantry and was equipped with three 3.7-inch mountain guns from India. These later saw service in the interior in 1955 and again 1957. Shortly after this, 75mm pack howitzers were acquired and in 1958 two 5.5-inch guns were borrowed from the British Army. During the Jebel

Artillery Troop training on 25-pounder guns in the early 1960s. (Muqaddam Ian Buttenshaw Collection)

Major Eddie Parks, SOA, in 1982, seen on the border between Oman and the PDRY. He is wearing a brown and green *shemagh* worn like a turban. (Major E. Parks Collection)

Akhdar Campaign the Artillery Troop manned a 75mm gun position at Tanuf and a 5.5-inch gun position at Kamah. The Artillery Troop expanded to a battery in 1960 with four 25-pounder guns, the two 5.5-inch guns were retained whilst the older guns were mothballed or disposed of. This quota of guns remained stable until after the start of the Dhofar War. The Artillery Training Centre was relocated to Suwaiq in December 1970, but the HQ remained in BAF. Two more batteries were raised in 1971, equipped with 25-pounder guns.

Re-designation of the artillery took place in 1971 when it was renamed Oman Artillery and two of the 75mm guns were brought back into service as a Light Air Portable Section, movable by helicopter. The same year the Oman Artillery moved to Rustaq and the Training Camp was disestablished at Suwaiq. India supplied a troop of 75/24 mm pack howitzers in 1972 which were retained until the end of hostilities. A Locating Troop using Cymbeline counter-mortar radar was formed in 1975. Another relocation for the Oman Artillery took effect in 1976 with a move to Izki and in the same year the 25-pounder guns started to be replaced by 105mm Light Guns, and the mountain guns, along with the Indian 75/24 mm pack howitzers, were phased-out, followed in 1977 by the 5.5-inch guns. Three batteries of 105mm Light Guns were introduced in 1976 and a further three batteries of the same were added later; by 1980 the Field Regiment had six batteries and a locating troop. During 1980 the Oman Artillery was re-designated Sultan of Oman's Artillery and the regiment was divided into 1SOA and 2SOA with each having three batteries. The same year two 130mm M-46 medium batteries were formed. A Low Level Air Defence Troop was also raised, fielding SA-7 MANPADs. Concurrent with the changes, the Locating Troop was enlarged to a battery and a Sound Ranging Troop, Artillery Intelligence Section and a Survey Troop were included. Blowpipe missiles were purchased and the AD Troop was expanded to an AD Battery. A third artillery regiment was raised in 1988 as a medium regiment (3SOA). 4 SOA was raised in 1992 in the air defence role. Modern equipment continued to be purchased upgrading the AD Regiment and the medium regiment.

UNIFORM AND REGALIA
A scarlet beret was worn by all SAF HQ officers and the Artillery Troop. A very dark navy blue square patch was worn behind the cap badge until 1986. The Artillery Troop also had the khaki *qulla* skull cap with red and yellow woollen *agal*, as did the Independent Guard until 1970, but without the yellow colour. Both units originated from the Muscat Regiment. The current artillery beret is royal blue. The original stable belt was originally red but at the time of writing is red over blue. The lanyard is white.

SAF ENGINEERS (SAFE)
Before the SAF Engineers were created the infantry battalion assault pioneer platoons carried out combat engineering tasks. Raised on 22 March 1974, the Sultan's Forces Engineers (SFE) Troop comprised two British Army officers, 2 British Army NCOs and 5 Omani NCOs that had completed an engineer course in Jordan. Thirty-three soldiers were accepted from the SAF Training Regiment and moved to Bait al Falaj for engineer training. The troop then went straight to Dhofar and came under the command of a British Royal Engineer squadron. A second troop was formed and trained by 1975 and Sultan's Force Engineers ran assault pioneer courses for the infantry battalions. The SFE worked with the British and Jordanian engineers with maintaining the Hornbeam Line and carried out road construction and mine clearance before operations. The SAF Engineer Squadron was at full strength in late 1975 and operational in 1976. In 1975, the route from Sarfait to Capstan was cleared of mines and the routes into the Sherishitti Caves were also cleared, enabling infantry to capture them. By 1976, the Engineer Squadron had an HQ and HQ Troop plus three Field Troops and a Support Troop. During 1977 the squadron was renamed Sultan of Oman's Armed Force Engineers (SAFE), and re-designated SAF Engineers Regiment in 1982. The structure of the regiment included a RHQ, 2 Field Squadrons and an Engineer Training School and a third squadron was added in 1986. The regiment was stationed at MAM with one squadron at Salalah. The HQ Squadron was raised at the beginning of the 1990s along with a Support Squadron. The emergence of an Armoured Engineer Squadron occurred in 1995 with the utilization of Panhard and Piranha armoured vehicles. Later in the decade M728 engineer tanks were added to the squadron. Growth continued, and 2 SAFE Regiment was created in 2008 by dividing the original large SAFE Regiment. Support for 23 Brigade was provided by 1 Combat Engineer Regiment which was located at MAM while 2 Combat Engineer Regiment was deployed to Salalah in support of 11 Brigade. 3 Engineer Regiment was later raised at MAM and became a General Support Regiment.

UNIFORM AND REGALIA
SAFE wear a chocolate brown beret and lanyard in chocolate brown with a double strand.

SAF SIGNALS (SAF SIGS)
A small signalling detachment was formed in 1955 in Bait al Falaj. A signals officer joined the detachment in 1958 and expanded the detachment to become a fully-fledged Signal Troop by 1961. In 1959, signalling courses were held at the Ghubra Training Centre before soldiers were posted to their unit. The Troop O.C. was a captain with the dual role of Force Signals Officer and Officer Commanding the Signal Troop. During 1962 a SAF telephone switchboard was established in BAF. A radio link was engineered in 1964 with the first SAF deployment to Dhofar, between UAG Barracks and BAF. TRA G40 transmitters and RW7 receivers were used for a Morse code circuit. In the field No.19 Wireless Sets were used which were carried by camel or donkey. The Salalah detachment was re-designated Southern Signal Troop by 1967. In the period 1968-73 there was a major upgrade in radio equipment, and private automatic branch exchanges were located at BAF, MAM and Muscat. New radio sets included BCC 30 manpack and C13s. Small automatic exchanges in the north were interfaced with the limited but expanding civil system. Both Northern Signal Troop and Southern Signal Troop, were expanded to squadron size in 1972, and by 1973/1974 along with a newly formed HQ Squadron,

which was located at BAF, became the Force Signal Regiment. A small Staff Branch was also added in BAF in 1974. Northern Oman Signal Squadron was divided into two in the same year. The operational elements were retained in Northern Oman Squadron and the newly raised Support Squadron contained the School of Signals, Base Radio Workshops, and the Quartermasters Troop. Northern Signal Squadron had Commcen Troops by 1977 at BAF and MAM, and a Line Troop. Detachments were located with the SAFTR, SOAF Seeb, Saiq, Khasab and Masirah. The squadron in Dhofar had troops in Salalah, Thumrait, Aydim (Manston), and a line troop. During 1977 all three services became independent, and the Signal Regiment was tasked with providing communications for SOLF at unit level, line communications for all three services, HF radios for SOAF, all crypto requirements for the MOD and the three services, the purchase of communications equipment for SOLF, provision of advice on ground communications to SOAF and SON, and the training of signals tradesmen. The Signal Regiment moved to MAM with all communications facilities in 1978. The School of Signals became a separate unit of the regiment and signallers for all three services underwent training there. From 1980, the School of Signals, Northern Oman Signal Squadron and HQ Signal Squadron were each commanded by an Omani officer and the first qualified Omani technicians joined the regiment in 1981. Although not officially established, the signals branch was functioning by 1982. The workload was too great for the regiment and consequently the Second Signal Regiment (2 Regiment Force Signals) was formed in 1985. A Force Telecommunication Equipment Workshop (FTEW) and Force Communications Equipment Depot (FCED) were established. The following year the post of Force Signals Officer was upgraded to Aqeed and a small HQ Force Signals established comprising Communications Coordinating Branch and Telephones Equipment Branch. The SAF School of Signals expanded to meet the growing demand for qualified communications personnel and became an independent sub-unit in January 1987. The title of Force Signals (F Sigs) was changed at some stage after the formation of Second Signal Regiment to SAF Sigs. Tropospheric scatter systems were introduced along with the latest communications technologies and advanced trunk communications in the field. Third Signal Regiment was raised in 2003 mainly to oversee static communications. In 2006, SAF Signals opened their new state-of-the-art School of Signals, concurrent with Project Gazelle 10, designed to develop SAF's strategic communications network throughout Oman.

UNIFORM AND REGALIA

A red beret was worn until 1974 when the colour changed to a medium blue beret, and a medium blue lanyard worn over the left shoulder. The first pattern signal headdress badge came out about 1970 having a white metal dagger as the central motif and a scroll on either side with the words Signal Battalion in Arabic. This was replaced with a new badge in 1981 with a gazelle's head. This was worn until 1988 with a blue felt backing in the shape of a square. At the same time that the second pattern badge was issued the Arabic-script white metal title "Services" on a red felt background, which was worn with the first badge, was replaced with a new white metal Arabic title *Kateeba al Asharra* (Signal Regiment) and abbreviated as *K.A. Sh* on the title. This was on an oblong blue felt backing.

FIRQAT (FQ)

The Firqat were paramilitary units raised from Surrendered Enemy Personnel (SEP). With the ascent of HM Sultan Qaboos, the Popular Front for the Liberation of Oman were offered amnesty and consequently many surrendered and were turned to fight for the Sultanate against their former communist masters. This was a sophisticated tactic learned by the British in Kenya and Malaya in the 1950s. The first group, named Firqat Salahadin (FSD), were trained by British Army Training Team (BATT) members from the SAS. The success of the Firqat was proven when, in 1971, they captured Sadh, a coastal village, after being dropped off by Coastal Patrol dhows, and turned even more enemy fighters after 140 of the Front's men wanted to join the Sultan. A total of 35 of them joined the FSD. Within a year there were 11 Firqats in operation. Each Firqat was managed by a team of 4 BATT members, whilst the size of the units themselves varied between 25 and 140 men. It was quickly realized that each Firqat had to consist of members of only one tribe. These small units excelled as guides, spotting enemy at distance, long range reconnaissance and raiding. A total of 29 Firqats were raised with a total strength of nearly 3,000 men. With the end of the war the Firqat was placed under the control of the Wali of Dhofar. Control was handed back to the SAF in 1977 as the Firqat still had military duties and the previous control had proved unsatisfactory. As the Firqat locations formed local hubs for the civilian population within their tribal areas it was decided to create more permanent Firqat posts and to create a formal Rural Security Force (RSF). Concurrent with the formation of the RSF was the establishing of a regular Oman Reconnaissance Force ORF (later re-designated Oman Reconnaissance Regiment ORR), which recruited younger men. The ORF became a professional force and a little detached from the Firqat; because of this it was decided to raise a Mobile Reserve Force (MRF) in 1984 and to recruit from RSF members. A target of 700 men was planned for 1989. The role of the MRF was to be able to provide a reservoir of troops competent and ready to serve when called upon to support the Land Force. As a rule the men were located in their assorted camps and came under command of HQ Rural Security Force. A small HQ for Firqat Forces was made available in June 1996, located next to Sahalnawt Camp. This was similar to a small brigade HQ and it was tasked with overseeing all Firqat duties and in addition provided training for all the Firqat Force at its training centre. The ORR became fully separate from the Firqat Force in the 1990s. The Rural Security Force title disappeared from use with the name Firqat Force being the accepted title. The posts in Dhofar were retained and consequently provided local intelligence for 11 Infantry Brigade.

UNIFORM AND REGALIA

The ORF wore a light green beret. ORF and ORR had worn a lime green triangular backing behind their cap badge before the 1986 patch was introduced.

MUSCAT REGIMENT (MR), MUSCAT LEVY CORPS (MLC) & MUSCAT INFANTRY (MI)

Around 1907, civilian Askars garrisoned in diverse forts of Muscat were given military training for the first time. Trouble was being stirred up in the interior and in 1913 dissident tribal forces captured Nizwa, Izki and Awabi. With this unrest Sultan Faisal bin Turki requested help from the British, which resulted in Indian troops being deployed to Muscat. Discussions were held in 1914 regarding a permanent force being created, however this was overtaken by an attack on Muscat by tribesmen from the interior during 1915. Known as the battle of Bait al Falaj, the enemy were soundly beaten off by the British-officered Indian troops. An agreement was signed at Al Sib (Seeb) in 1920 and the Muscat Levy Corps was raised in 1921.

Table 15: Overview of the MR, MLC & MI, 1921-1957

Period	Name
1921-1931	Muscat Levy Corps
1931-1957	Muscat Infantry
1957-	Muscat Regiment

MUSCAT LEVY CORPS (MLC)

Former soldiers of the Seistan Levy Corps from Persian Baluchistan were commanded by Captain E D McCarthy. They arrived at Matrah, Oman, in 1921 and were named the Muscat Levy Corps (MLC). Due to the soldiers suffering sickness in the Omani climate they were all replaced by the middle of 1922 with Makrani Baluch from Gwadar, the Sultanate's enclave. A few Arabs and Africans also joined the Levy. Captain McCarthy was replaced in 1923 by Captain R G E W Alban. The Levy was 2-300 men strong and was more suited to garrison duties than active soldiering. Their role was to provide armed guards for the Sultan's Palace, Sultanate Treasury, and the British Political Agency. Two 2.75-inch screw guns were sent to the MLC in the late 1920s. J E Petersons book *Oman Insurgencies* mentions that the Sultan requested a pipe band.

MUSCAT INFANTRY (MI)

The Muscat Levy Corps was renamed the Muscat Infantry in 1931 and combined military exercises with HMS *Fowey* took place in 1937. The MI became run down during the 1930s due to lack of funding and was barely over 150 men in strength, even so the structure of the MI included an HQ company and an A and B Company, albeit understrength. Later additional guard duties were required for al Jalali and al-Mirani and later still the British Bank of the Middle East. An Artillery Troop was formed within the Muscat Infantry in 1942, and three 3.7-inch guns were added to the Artillery Troop that same year. By 1956 the Muscat Infantry had 1 British officer, 1 Pakistan officer and 185 other ranks. The unit was organised as listed in Table 16. The Muscat Infantry was re-designated Muscat Regiment in 1957.

Table 16: Muscat Infantry, 1956

Element	Equipment	Notes
HQ Company		incl. Artillery Section (three 3.7-inch howitzers, three 2.75-inch screw guns)
Two Rifle Companies		
Medium Machine Gun Section	Four Vickers medium machine guns	
Signal Section		
Motor Transport Section		
Administrative Section		

UNIFORM RANK AND REGALIA

The Muscat Infantry wore the Indian Army uniform and ranks. The cap badge of the Muscat Infantry was the emblem of the Sultan of Oman which consisted of a *Khunjah* (or Omani dagger of Al Said

Muscat Infantry headdress badge on red background. Officers had their brass badges silvered. (Cliff Lord collection)

Muscat Regiment red Tam o' Shanter with silver officer's cap badge. (Cliff Lord Collection)

family pattern) superimposed on crossed *Saifs* (or Omani tribal swords). The scroll read 1 Muscat Infantry. The headdress badge was made in brass and with a silver wash for officers. A brass shoulder title was worn with the word MUSCAT straight and a curved word INFANTRY below.

Table 17: Ranks of the Muscat Infantry

Rank	British Equivalent
Subedar Major	Major
Subedar	Lieutenant
Jemadar	2nd Lieutenant
Havildar	Sergeant
Naik	Corporal
Sepoy	Soldier

MUSCAT REGIMENT (MR)

The Sultan's Armed Forces (SAF) superseded the Muscat Armed Forces (MAF) in the major reorganisation of military forces in 1957. The purpose of the change was to make the military more professional and fit for purpose. Muscat Infantry was renamed the Muscat Regiment and the establishment was upgraded.

During the recapture of the interior in August 1957, Haugh Force — commanded by Lt Col. Frank Haugh — was raised from the MR and sent from Muscat to Wadi Sumail, and captured Mutti, a rebel stronghold while on the way to meet up with Carter Force. Carter Force, commanded by Lieutenant Colonel Stewart Carter of the Trucial Oman Scouts, left Izki to relocate to Birkat al Mawz and to join Haugh Force. Other units captured Nizwa but some of the rebels escaped and relocated to the secure fastness of Jebel Akhdar (Green Mountain) with supplies reaching them through Aswad and Awabi. From their mountaintop the rebels were able to cause trouble by raiding and mining roads. The MR sent troops to invest Aswad and Awabi with the task to interdict the passage

A lance corporal of the Muscat Regiment wearing khaki *qulla* and red and yellow wool *agal*, around 1960. (Muqaddam Ian Buttenshaw Collection)

Captain Berty Bowes of the Muscat Regiment, in the early 1960s, wearing the regimental Tam o' Shanter. (Courtesy Eddie Parks)

of arms and supplies to the rebels and block off the north of the Jebel. In November 1958, while patrolling they discovered a hidden route to the mountain via Wadi Hijar. This route was later used by the British SAS and a platoon of the MR to obtain a foothold on the mountain. A platoon of MR remained until the assault on the mountain was completed successfully. In May 1965, A and B Companies plus half of HQ Company were flown to Dhofar to clear 60 dissidents where they successfully captured 20 men and a large stockpile of weapons and ammunition. The regiment played an important part in the Dhofar war, including participation in Operation Hadaf and the location known as *Capstan* — a codename name given by the troops for a rocky and prominent feature to be found half way down the escarpment towards the sea near Sarfait — and taken by them, isolating the dissidents from their supplies from the Peoples' Democratic Republic of Yemen. In the Sarfait area there were three positions in the mountains, in addition to *Capatan*, there was *Mainbrace*, and *Yardarm*. *Mainbrace* was on the edge of the escarpment and was the HQ for the Sarfait position. MR also took part in the successful action at Darra Ridge in 1975 where they joined up with the Frontier Force. Later they were to become the first motorized regiment in 1982, and subsequently the second mechanised infantry regiment.

Two vehicles of the Muscat Regiment with their red TAC sign on the front of the vehicles. On the left is a Mowag Piranha II and on the right is a Panhard Véhicule Blindé Léger (light armoured vehicle). (Courtesy: Muqaddam Ian Buttenshaw)

UNIFORM AND REGALIA

Other ranks wore a khaki drill *qulla* with a red and yellow *agal* attached. A red patch was worn behind the cap badge on the khaki Forstmeister peaked cap. In 1957 a red Tam o' Shanter hat with a red toorie was introduced. The headdress was modelled on the hat worn by the British Army's Cameronian Regiment, which assisted in the recapture of Nizwa. The old Sultan, when thanking the Cameronian CO, admired his hat and said that his senior regiment would wear the same but in red, the colour of the then Oman flag. When Sultan Qaboos was asked which UK regiment he would like to serve in for a year in 1962, he is alleged to have chosen the Cameronians. The scarlet Tam o' Shanter thus became the distinguishing headdress for the Muscat Regiment, with the cap badge with a red silk ribbon behind it worn on the left side over the ear. Officer's pips were silver-coloured five-pointed stars. A brass 'MR' was worn on each shoulder, this was changed to Arabic calligraphy by about 1963-64, and was made in white metal for officers and brass for other ranks. Other ranks only wore the Tam o' Shanter on drill parades and formal occasions. The *qulla* was discontinued immediately Sultan Qaboos took over in 1970 and was replaced with a plain red beret. A red and white *shemagh* was also worn on occasion when travelling in vehicles, which were all open topped. All ranks were issued with a black *agal*, which should have been worn Trucial Oman Scouts style, but in practise the *shemagh* was wrapped around the face to minimise sand getting into the mouth, ears and nose when travelling. MR's *shemagh* was worn up to at least 1967 during the Dhofar campaign, after which the entire army moved to a green and black *shemagh* worn in a turban style. A scarlet stable belt was worn by all officers in the Armed Forces. Other ranks wore red hose tops for parades. Officers' uniforms in the early 1960s consisted of khaki drill shirts, bush jackets, whipcord slacks, khaki drill slacks, desert boots or *chaplis* (sandals). This uniform was also worn by the NFR but with a green beret and HQ SAF with a scarlet beret. All wore the Force cap badge.

BATINAH FORCE (BF) & NORTHERN FRONTIER REGIMENT (NFR)

The BF was formed at Sohar in January 1953 to protect the northern frontiers. Major Colin Maxwell was the first commanding officer with Captain St John Armitage as his 2IC. By April, only 50 men had joined the force but this increased to 120 all ranks by the end of the year. The force was comprised of Arabs and two British officers, and was organised as per a standard British Army rifle company. Weapons included Rifles Mk.4, Bren LMGs, 2-inch mortars, and hand grenades. Transport consisted of Land Rovers and Bedford 3-ton lorries. There was no link to the Muscat Infantry as the latter were Baluch and spoke Urdu. Batinah Force was raised with normal

British unit standards and discipline and with words of command given in Arabic.

By 1954 the force was trained, operational and military posts were created on the northern frontier and on the route from Buraimi to the coast. The second in command, Captain St John Armitage, was transferred to Salalah in 1954 to raise the Dhofar Force, and was later replaced by another British officer, Captain D.C. Pope. A Training Depot was formed at Ghobra (Ghallah) in 1955 and a second company was raised and trained for the defence of Buraimi. The BF first saw action in 1955 when it was deployed to capture the fort at Aswad which had been occupied by men from the Trucial States. Eighty enemy were driven off by the BF with the enemy suffering some casualties. Also in 1955, the BF re-occupied Rustaq after being heavily engaged by the rebel forces in the Hazm area. The force was about 200 strong by the end of 1956 and consisted of a HQ and 2 rifle companies, with the HQ at Sohar, and one company at Buraimi Oasis. With the reorganization of the MAF in 1957, Batinah Force was re-designated Northern Frontier Regiment, and became at that time the second regiment in seniority after the MR. Also in 1957, A Company moved to Fahud with B Company and TAC HQ joining later. They were involved in the recapture of Nizwa as part of Carter Force. A third company was raised towards the end of the same year when the former members of the disbanded OR joined the regiment. NFR were involved in the Jebel Akhdar campaign and took part in the successful assault on the mountain. The regiment built a permanent Camp at Saiq with its tactical advantage of overlooking the plateau.

NFR was the first regiment to serve in Dhofar and in 1964 they deployed a company to Ayn Arzat. From there it patrolled throughout Dhofar for a year, with no contacts, before returning to the north of Oman. Red Company, known as the Desert Corps, was formed within the regiment in 1965/1966 with a role to reinforce the SAF when necessary. A year later, in 1966, the regiment returned south to camp at Umm al-Gawariff located near Salalah. Some members of the Dhofar Force tried unsuccessfully to assassinate Sultan Said while on tour in April 1966. As a result of this the NFR were called in and disarmed Dhofar Force (see Dhofar Force). During the Dhofar War the NFR rotated into the region every-other year. Regimental Colours were presented to the regiment on 16 November 1974. The unit also served in Operation Desert Storm in February 1991 in the Liberation of Kuwait as part of the Saudi Arabian Brigade.

UNIFORM AND REGALIA (BF)

BF uniform and equipment was as per British Army tropical issue. Khaki drill shirts and slacks or shorts were worn and troops were issued with green hose tops, green lanyards and a green beret. Rifle Brigade Green was the regimental colour.

Table 18: Overview of the BF & NFR

Period	Name
1953-1957	Batinah Force
1957-	Northern Frontier Regiment

UNIFORM AND REGALIA (NFR)

The NFR wore rifle green berets showing their link with Batinah Force. Officers in the early 1960s had a red patch behind the beret badge, which they retained until the RAO badge was introduced. A green patch was worn behind the cap badge of the Forstmeister cap. A green and dark brown *shemagh* was worn. The NFR shoulder title was introduced in 1957 and was made of copper using the Roman

A patrol of the Northern Frontier Regiment in 1966. The officer has long trousers while the men wear shorts. 1937 pattern webbing, blancoed white, is worn. (Muqaddam Ian Buttenshaw Collection)

Northern Frontier Regiment Officer and men at Muscat circa 1960s. (By kind permission of J E Peterson from the Malcolm G Dennison Photograph Collection)

GKN Piranha II, introduced in 1996 and delivered to the Desert Regiment. These had a 7.62mm GPMG mounted on the cupola, and were later retrofitted with a locally made turret, mounting a Browning .50 on troop carrying APCs. Other variants retained the GPMG on the cupola. (Courtesy: Muqaddam Ian Buttenshaw)

letters NFR. This Pakistani-made title was used very briefly after the Batinah Force was re-designated and was replaced after a couple of years or less, with an Arabic script shoulder title with a green underlay. A Rifle Green woven double strand lanyard is worn.

DESERT REGIMENT (DR)

The Desert Regiment was third in seniority and originated in part with Red Company of the NFR as it formed the nucleus of the regiment in 1966. A second company was raised with soldiers from NFR, MR, and the Oman Gendarmerie (OG) and it also contained men from the SAFTC, the Baluch Training Company. A third company was raised in 1967 which brought the regiment up to full strength. The Desert Regiment served in Dhofar during the war and took part in many operations. These included Operation Simba where they captured Sarfait on the Yemen border in April 1972, and Operation Diana. Operation Diana was launched by the SAF to install small units on the edge of Jebel to enable the Firqat to mount patrols and respond to any firing of mortars or rockets, and ultimately deny the Adoo their firing positions. Regimental Colours were presented in 1975. The Ahmed Bin Said Camp was opened in December 1983 for the Desert Regiment. During 1985 the unit was the first to be converted into a mechanised infantry regiment. Mobilization occurred in 2003, for participation in the Island Shield Force and the regiment was despatched to Kuwait to strengthen their defences against Iraq in March and retuned in May that year.

UNIFORM AND REGALIA

Sand Yellow coloured beret worn. Lanyard is sand yellow single strand.

THE JEBEL REGIMENT (JR)

Formed in 1970, the Jebel Regiment was the fourth infantry regiment. Initially located in Bid Bid camp, the regiment attained full strength in 1971 and deployed to Dhofar, returning to Nizwa in 1972. The unit was again posted to Dhofar in 1973, being camped at Sarfait, and later returned north. The regiment took part in the attack on the Sherishitti Caves in 1975 before returning to Nizwa. Regimental Colours were presented on 1 November 1975 by HM The Sultan. A final tour of Dhofar was at Sarfait in 1976 and remained there until the end of hostilities. The regiment later converted to the motorized infantry regiment role. A move to Nizwa Camp took place in 1980.

UNIFORM AND REGALIA

Grey beret worn. Before the RAO badge was introduced a black diamond was worn behind the regimental badge. The lanyard is woven grey double strand.

OMAN COAST REGIMENT (OCR), OMAN GENDARMERIE (OG), OIL INSTALLATION POLICE (OIPOG) AND OIL INSTALLATION GUARD (OIP)

The Oman Gendarmerie was formed in June 1959 at Bait Kashmir in Sohar. Its intended role was for it to be used as a rural armed constabulary to relieve the burden of the SAF infantry regiments on the northern borders and Batinah coast to prevent smuggling, gun running and to assist with customs checks at border posts. Initially the Oman Gendarmerie was conceived to be a company-size unit of 120 men to be able to mingle with the people and provide intelligence. However, events saw the OG quickly grow into a much larger unit.

The OG was comprised of troops and were deployed to posts, which came under the Sector HQ. In 1960 the HQ moved to Azaiba near Muscat and in May of that year, Major Jasper Coates of the OG raised the Coastal Patrol which was tasked with patrolling the Batinah coast. The first dhow was named *Nasr al Bahr* and two more dhows were added from 1966. This was the antecedent of the Sultan of Oman's Navy (SON) in 1971. During 1962 the HQ OG moved to Seeb and HQ Western Sector was established at Buraimi. By 1963 the OG had a strength of 253 men with troops located as listed in Table 19. The sectors became squadrons in 1972. There were never more than six squadrons, all under Commander OG at Seeb, all with their allocated sectors.

In 1970 OG was required to provide guards and bodyguards for Sultan Qaboos and OG Palace Sector (PALSEC) was raised in August of that year. PALSEC replaced the MUSGAR Guard Company which protected the palaces and Treasury. Bodyguard responsibility was relinquished in 1972 and PALSEC was renamed F Squadron OG and became responsible for the external protection of palaces. In 1973 the Royal Guard Squadron was formed from F Squadron OG. Northern Oman Border Scouts (NOBS) was established in 1974 under command of the OG and transferred to the Royal Oman Police in 1976.

A parachute unit was raised by D Squadron OG in 1975 and training took place in Saudi Arabia. On return to Oman the unit was re-designated D (PARA) Squadron (OPS) and became an independent unit. US-made BGM-71 TOW anti-tank guided missiles were received by the OG in 1975 to strengthen the positions on the Yemen border. Later in 1976 they were transferred to the Armoured Car Squadron which formed a TOW anti-

Panhard Véhicule Blindé Léger (light armoured vehicle), or VBL. 132 were initially supplied, with eight capable of mounting the US-made TOW ATGM. This example has the FN-H MAG GPMG mounted. (Courtesy: Muqaddam Ian Buttenshaw)

tank troop with weapons mounted on Land Rovers.

Table 19: Bases of the OG, 1962-1966

Sector	Bases & Notes
North Sector (NORSEC)	Sohar, Aswad, Khatmat Milahah
West Sector (WESSEC)	Buraimi, Mahdah, Qabil
Central Sector (CENSEC)	Seeb, Suwaiq
Palace Sector (PALSEC)	est. 1970; Muscat; re-designated F Squadron in 1972; re-assigned to the RG in 1973
Peninsular Sector (PENSEC)	est. 1971; Khasab, Musandam
South Sector (SOUSEC)	est. 1971; Sur

During the Dhofar campaign troops were sent to guard static locations on occasion, including the Yemen border, notably Habrut. The OG also served on the Salalah Plain. In 1974 OG picquetted the Midway Road and was assisted by the Royal Guard Squadron. OG continued to patrol all over Oman, particularly the northern borders, and from early 1971 the Southern Sector (SOUSEC) base at Sur.

The Second in Command of the OG was transferred to the Muscat Police in 1969 as commissioner, while the SAFTC trained the first recruits for this revamped police force. The requirement of the OG was lessened with the growth of the Royal Oman Police and on 1 January 1978 OG was re-designated as the Oman Coast Regiment.

UNIFORM AND REGALIA
Blue *mazri* shirt and khaki long trousers. Blue and white *shemagh* and black *agal*. Dark blue lanyard. Standard SAF headdress badge worn.

OIL INSTALLATION POLICE, OMAN GENDARMERIE & OIL INSTALLATION GUARD
In the 1960s the OG raised a unit to defend the oil company exploration teams. Called the 'Oil Installation Police, Oman Gendarmerie', this was paid for by the Petroleum Development Oman (PDO) oil company, and trained and administered by the OG. This unit was renamed the Oil Installation Guard in the early 1970s and was transferred to the Royal Oman Police in 1974.

UNIFORM AND REGALIA
The OIPOG and OIG wore a similar uniform to the OG (blue shirt and khaki long trousers) but wore a red and white chequered *shemagh*. The standard SAF headdress badge was worn.

ADDF SUPPORT TO THE OMAN GENDARMERIE
The OG responsibilities were excessive and consequently they were over-committed with their manpower. Duties included manning their sectors and also providing units for service in Dhofar. Two rifle squadrons of the Abu Dhabi Defence Force were stationed in Sohar from October 1973 to January 1974 and from November 1974 to April 1975. This enabled the OG from Sohar to be deployed to Dhofar.

OMAN COAST REGIMENT (OCR)
The Oman Coast Regiment (OCR) was created on 1 January 1978 as a result of the conversion of the Oman Gendarmerie to an infantry regiment. The regiment's squadrons were re-designated as companies to conform to its new infantry regiment role and the OG roles were gradually relinquished. The OCR initially had

Captain J. J. Gerrard BEM DSM, in the uniform of the Oman Gendarmerie, around 1970. (Muqaddam Ian Buttenshaw Collection)

OG manning a 106mm RCL at Makinat Shihan in Dhofar. They are wearing their olive green kit. (Muqaddam Ian Buttenshaw Collection)

Group of OG Soldiers after the first National Day Parade on 23 July 1971. They are wearing dark blue and white chequered *shemagh* with a black *agal*, dark blue shirt and khaki trousers. (Muqaddam Ian Buttenshaw Collection)

responsibility for NORSEC (Sohar), WESSEC (Buraimi) and PENSEC (Musandam) with the RHQ and HQ Squadron was located at Seeb; SOUSEC at Sur became the Navy Training Centre; CENSEC at Batinah was taken over by the Jebel Regiment. The regiment moved to Bid Bid for re-training as an infantry regiment and was obliged to participate in deployments to Dhofar and spent time in Sarfait. A permanent base for the regiment was found in 1983 at Buraimi and Sohar camps. During August 1990, a company was on ISF duties at Hafar al Batin when Iraq invaded Kuwait.

Oman Oil Installation Guard, formerly the Oil Installation Police, in the early 1970s. (Muqaddam Ian Buttenshaw)

The remainder of the battalion joined the company, along with artillery support and anti-tank forces, within the GCCs section of the Coalition Force though before any military action took place the regiment was relieved by the NFR. The OCR and Northern Frontier Regiment were paired in 2001 and did a three-yearly rotation between Arzat in the south and Buraimi/Sohar in the north.

UNIFORM AND REGALIA

Black and blue woven single strand lanyard. Black beret with royal blue square badge backing.

SULTAN OF OMAN'S PARACHUTE (SO PARA)

Parachuting started in Oman with D (PARA) Squadron Oman Gendarmerie when in 1974 it was decided to raise a parachutist unit. A year later three groups of volunteers were sent to Tabuk in Saudi Arabia for parachutist training. Training continued until the Parachute Training School was established at Maabela in 1977. In 1978, D Squadron became an independent unit, known as Oman Parachute Squadron (OPS), within Northern Oman Brigade. The reason for the name change was because the Oman Gendarmerie had been converted to the infantry role and the OPS needed to grow. A move to Rustaq was undertaken by the squadron and the Parachute Training School during 1979 where a National Free Fall Team was formed in 1980 from members of the OPS. The team is reputed to have had a very high standard of training and participated in a number of international competitions and attained high positions. Milan anti-tank weapons were provided to OPS and it was the only unit in the army to receive them in 1982, showing confidence in the unit which was fast becoming regimental size. With a HQ and 2 squadrons with a parachutist and anti-tank role it was retitled Oman Parachute Regiment (OPR). This title remained until 1985 when the regiment was re-designated Sultan of Oman's Parachute Regiment (SOPR). Regimental Colours were presented on 10 December 1987. The regiment's Milan anti-tank troop supported the Land Force contingent in Saudi Arabia and Kuwait from 8 August 1990 to 1 July 1991. In 1993, the regiment was re-named and became known as the Sultan of Oman's Parachute (SO Para). TOW anti-tank missiles on Land Cruisers were transferred from the MSO in 1994 making a third squadron. French-made Panhard light armoured vehicles fitted with TOW ATGMs were introduced in 1997 and provided an increased support capability

with these additional anti-tank weapons. SO Para provided support to the DR Battle Group within the GCC operations in Kuwait from March to May 2003.

UNIFORM AND REGALIA

A dark grey beret and a maroon double strand lanyard is worn. A maroon flash was placed behind the beret badge, and maroon sliders were worn over the epaulets. The stable belt is dark grey with a single maroon stripe. Whilst a maroon beret almost universally signifies a parachute unit, the maroon beret is not worn in the RAO because when the OC D (PARA) proposed this colour to HM during his first visit, HM refused as he wanted his new Royal Guard Regiment to wear maroon, which they still do.

BALUCH GUARD (BG) & FRONTIER FORCE (FF)

The Baluch Guard (BG) was raised in 1971 by Lt Col Vyvyan Robinson MC and Lt Khuda Bux, both coming from the MR. The Baluch Guard was a second line force of about 700 or more men in 17 platoons. Its role was to provide detachments and platoons for static positions, e.g. the hedgehog fortifications on the Salalah Plain, and holding ground captured by the infantry battalions. By taking on these tasks they relieved infantry battalions from these less-demanding tasks and enabled them to concentrate on aggressive soldiering. The BG performed a similar task to the Dhofar Gendarmerie but was not as well equipped. While based at Raysut, due to their allegiance to both the Wali of Dhofar and the HQ Dhofar Brigade, its elements were usually attached to the Guards and different combat units – especially so during Operation Jaguar in October 1971. In January 1973, the Baluch Guard was converted into a regular SAF regiment and re-named as the Frontier Force (FF).

FRONTIER FORCE

Raised in 1973 from the Baluch Guard, Frontier Force was tasked with protecting the western border. In 1973 the FF moved into positions on the Hornbeam Line and later moved to Sarfait before returning to the Eastern Jebel. Following this there was a return to the Hornbeam Line in 1974 where they had a successful operation in the Wadi Ashawq while on Operation Himar. The seven-company force under FF also contained companies from the KJ, DR and JR. Their task was to locate and attack the Front's 9th June Regiment's positions in Wadi Ashwaq, which was in the Hornbeam Line area. The enemy regimental HQ was captured and large amounts of ammunition collected, including a Katyushka rocket launcher. After Himar there was no further permanent enemy forces in the area. The Frontier Force were also involved in Operation Hadaf in 1975 against the Sherishitti Caves, and later that year in Operation Hilwah clearing the Darra Ridge. This enabled them to join up with the MR from Sarfait. The Frontier Force was entirely Baluch and remained in Dhofar until 1997 when all the Baluch infantry were transferred to the WFR and replaced with Omani personnel. They were paired up with the KJ. Regimental Colours were presented by HM Sultan Qaboos on 4 October 1976.

UNIFORM AND REGALIA

Khaki beret worn. Lanyard khaki woven double strand.

DHOFAR FORCE (DF), DHOFAR GENDARMERIE (DG), SOUTHERN REGIMENT/KATEEBA JANOOB (KJ) AND SOUTHERN OMAN REGIMENT/KATEEBA JANOOB OMAN (KJ)

Dhofar Force, which was formed in 1955, was an independent force separate from the MAF and SAF. However, in 1970 it became a part of the SAF and was renamed as the Dhofar Gendarmerie. The DG was tasked to carry out patrols on the Salalah Plain. Dhofar Gendarmerie was re-designated as Southern Regiment (KJ) in January 1974, and located near Salalah. Ian Buttenshaw explains in his book *The Royal Army of Oman and its Units: A Brief History* that the regiment used the Arab initials for *Kateeba Janoob* instead of the letters SR so that it would not be confused with Signal Regiment. KJ was an all Baluch unit. During the Dhofar War the regiment spent most of its operational time on the Jebel and was based at Sarfait. The title was changed to *Kateeba Janoob Oman* (Southern Oman Regiment) in 1990, however it was still referred to as KJ. From 1996, the regiment replaced most of its Baluch solders with Omanis and the Baluch were transferred to the WFR. It became paired with the FF. Regimental Colours were presented on 4 October 1976.

UNIFORM AND REGALIA

Dark green beret worn with burnt orange badge backing. Lanyard dark green and burnt orange double strand woven.

Recruits of the Dhofar Force on training during the late 1950s. (Muqaddam Ian Buttenshaw Collection)

WESTERN FRONTIER REGIMENT (WFR)

WFR owes its origin to several sources including the Dhofar Guard Unit which had provided a static guard at Thumrait Camp (Midway) and another at Aydim (Manston). There was also Z Company of the MUSGAR which provided a mobile force guarding and patrolling the Salalah Plains. Once hostilities ceased there was no requirement

Dhofar Force shoulder title. (Eddie Parks Collection)

Headdress badge of the Dhofar Force. (Cliff Lord Collection)

Collar badge of the Dhofar Force (Eddie Parks Collection)

A belt buckle worn by one of the very few officers that served 1955-1970 in the small unit known as Dhofar Force. It was not a part of Muscat Armed Forces and its successor the Sultans Armed Forces. DF was directly controlled by the Sultan. (Eddie Parks Collection)

for the Dhofar Guard or Z Company and it was decided to group them into a new regiment to be known as the Western Frontier Regiment, which was raised in 1976 at Thumrait. WFR was an all Baluch unit taking in some Baluch soldiers from other regiments, in particular from the Frontier Force and KJ. WFR was responsible for territory from the Saudi border to Habrut on the Yemen border. An incursion in 1987 by the PDRY into Dhofar resulted in 2 men killed and 8 captured. Operation Saif was conducted to regain the correct borders of Oman once again, an action in which WFR played an important part. United Press International reported that the Yemeni incursion was a misunderstanding. The Regimental Colours were presented by HM Sultan Qaboos in 1978.

UNIFORM AND REGALIA

The WFR wore a lime-green beret and a green underlay under their white metal shoulder titles. Lime-green double strand lanyard.

OMAN RECONNAISSANCE REGIMENT (ORR)

Originating from the experimental Operations Company in the RSF in 1979, a second company was raised in 1980 and they were renamed Mobile Firqat Force (MFF) which became a reconnaissance unit using Land Rovers. They were re-designated Oman Reconnaissance Force (ORF) in 1983 and became a highly trained force which by 1984 included a third company. On 13 May 1989 the ORF was renamed Oman Reconnaissance Regiment (ORR) and was tasked to provide recce support to the RAO in the form of the Screen Force with the CSF and WBSF and was also to provide civil aid to the people of the mountains if required. The regiment was stationed at Sahalnawt Cliffs Camp adjacent to Firqat Forces HQ.

UNIFORM AND REGALIA
Light green beret worn.

WESTERN BORDER SECURITY FORCE (WBSF)
With the demise of the OG and its conversion to an infantry regiment in 1978, a vacuum was left that required new units to be raised to cover some of the OG's former duties. On 1 December 1980, the WBSF was stood up as an independent unit of Northern Oman Brigade and tasked as a vehicle-borne reconnaissance company. Raised at MAM, the WBSF relocated to Qabil where it was responsible for patrolling the borders in the Qabil area, and in wartime working with the ORR and CSF forming part of the Screen Force. The duties of the WBSF were to patrol the western border area using mobile patrols, which were also known as "desert groups", visiting villages where they were able to provide civil aid to the people and also gain intelligence of the area.

UNIFORM AND REGALIA
The WBSF wore the green/khaki Tam o' Shanter style hat from 1983, with a large badge on the side. Prior to this they wore the SOLF *shemagh*. When all troops changed to SOLF badges, a dark khaki-green beret was worn with a ribbon rosette of the same colour. Lanyard green khaki double strand.

EAST COAST SECURITY FORCE & COASTAL SECURITY FORCE (CSF)
Raised in January 1981 in MAM, the force was known as the East Coast Security Force, which was an independent force under the command of Northern Oman Brigade. Recruitment was from the Sharqiah area and the patrol area was from Tiwi to Filim and also included a considerable part of the Wahiba Sands. Re-designation to Coastal Security Force was implemented in August 1981. Relocation to new barracks at Ibra took place where they were co-located with the DR. Another relocation occurred in 1987 when the CSF moved to Sur. The mission of the unit is to act as a reconnaissance company with their role in wartime to be a part of the Screen Force with the ORR and WBSF. Under normal conditions the role is to patrol its area of responsibility.

UNIFORM AND REGALIA
The CSF wore the green/khaki Tam o' Shanter style hat, with a large badge on the left side, until all troops changed to SOLF Badges, when a dark khaki green beret was worn with a ribbon rosette of the same colour. Lanyard green khaki double strand.

MUSANDAM SECURITY FORCE (MSF)
Raised in 1980 from members of the Shihu tribe, the company sized force was tasked to carry out patrols from its headquarters in Bukha throughout the Musandam peninsular coast and mountains. The original recruits were sent to the SAFTR and completed training on 4 September 1980. The MSF established themselves into Bukha Fort relieving a company of the Desert Regiment on 6 September 1980 and placed its HQ there. Other positions were taken over from the Peninsular Reinforcement Battalion (PRB) company as other platoons were trained and eventually the PRB withdrew. The MSF came under the command of HQ Musandam Sector, formerly HQ PENSEC, and did not deploy outside of Musandam. Encampments included Bukha, Wadi Bih, Dibba (Bayah), and Limah. The force's strength was increased from 2004 to a small battalion size and consisted of a small battalion HQ, two companies and logistic support elements. Battalion HQ and one company were located at Bukha and the second company was located at Khasab and later a third company was formed at Dibba.

UNIFORM AND REGALIA
The MSF wore the green Tam o' Shanter style hat with a large badge on the side until all troops changed to SOLF badges. A dark khaki-green beret is worn with a ribbon rosette of the same colour. Lanyard green khaki double strand. The MSF did not wear a white metal shoulder title before the universal title was issued for all units.

SULTAN'S ARMED FORCES TRAINING REGIMENT (SAFTR)
Military training started in 1955 when a training cell was formed at Ghallah Camp, and in 1962 became the SAF Training Centre. Three squads were trained each year with the course lasting 16 weeks. The centre was retitled SAF Training Regiment in 1971 and provided basic training for all three services. Also in 1971 a Potential Officers Training Wing was founded. Further to this, wings were formed to provide drill, weapon, support weapon, and NCO tactics instruction. The Potential Officers Training Wing was relocated to Aydim during 1981 and became the independent WTM. In 1985, the Support Weapons and Tactics Wing relocated to Aydim, but remained under the SAFTR. The following year all units came under one headquarters and consequently the KSQA was built which included a wing for Officer Cadets and another for Support Weapon and SNCO Tactics Courses. The Jebel Akhdar Battle Training Centre later came under the SAFTR command.

JEBEL AKHDAR BATTLE TRAINING CAMP (JABTC)
A Northern Frontier Regiment Company was located on the Jebel Akhdar in 1959 to establish a permanent military force there, and to ensure security within the area. In 1975 the establishment of the cadre for the Battle Training Centre was approved and came under HQ Northern Military Command. The camp was for the use of all regiments and units and provides training assistance and training programmes. JABTC came under HQ SOLF (Training Branch) in 1986 until the mid-1990s when it transferred to the SAFTR.

Table 20: Antecedents of the Sultan Qaboos Military Academy (Koliyat Sultan Qaboos al-Askariya, KSQA)

Period	Designation
1971-1981	Potential Officer Training Wing (SAFTR)
1981-1986	Potential Officer Training Unit (WTM)
1986-	Sultan Qaboos Military Academy (KSQA)
	including: Officer Cadet Wing, *Madrassat Tadreeb al-Murashaheen*, (MTM)
	including: Support Weapons and Tactics School, *Madrassat Tadreeb Aslihat Al-Isnad al-Wa'A'Tabia*, (MTS)

In 1971, the first training course was held at the Potential Officer Training Wing at Ghallah. The wing moved to Aydim Training Centre in Dhofar in 1981 and was renamed Potential Officer Training Unit *Wahadat Tadreeb Al Murashaheen*, (WTM). HM the Sultan changed the title to Sultan Qaboos Military Academy or *Koliyat Sultan Qaboos al Askariya* (KSQA) in 1986. Within the KSQA were two wings: *Madrassat Tadreeb al-Murashaheen* (MTM) which caters for officer cadets and *Madrassat Tadreeb Aslihat Al-Isnad al-Wa'A'Tabia* (MTS) which specialises in support weapons and tactics.

OFFICERS TRAINING SCHOOL, MADRASAT TADREEB A'DHUBAT, (MTD)

The Officers Training School *Madrasat Tadreeb A'Dhubat* (MTD) history starts with the Command Training Centre raised in June 1978 at MAM Camp. Advanced courses were provided to company commander level. The centre was moved to Sohar in July 1983 and was reorganised to become an officer training school capable of providing courses up to regimental commander's level. It was renamed MTD.

THE COMMAND AND STAFF COLLEGE

The Command and Staff College held its first course on 30 September 1987. The Staff College's role was to train officers in joint command and staff duties related to the topography and operational situation in the Sultanate of Oman. The unit came under the Office of COSSAF.

FORCE MEDICAL SERVICES (FMS)

Force Medical Services trace their roots back to 1920 when a small medical team with limited facilities was established at BAF. While this unit remained operational until at least 1958, in the early 1960s two medical centres were established. One was with the Muscat Regiment and the other with the Northern Frontier Regiment. By 1967 the medical training centre was moved to BAF and a clinic opened in UAG in the same year with 8 beds. During 1969 the medical services was known as Force Medical Unit. Re-designation took place 1 January 1973 when the Force Medical Unit became the Force Medical Services. The Medical Services continued to grow to meet the requirements of the times with building of hospitals and medical centres for military personnel and their families. A Forces Base Hospital was opened in MAM in 1974, followed in 1980 with a Forces Medical Equipment Depot. Casualty Clearing Posts were introduced in 1983 and a Field Surgical Team added in 1993. The Armed Forces Hospital at Al Khoudh was opened in 1985 with 175 beds. Specialist treatment is available to members of the Omani population. The Medical Training School opened in the 1980s was upgraded in 2005 and provided with new purpose-built accommodation. A Field Hospital was added to the FMS in 2008 and the Casualty Clearance Station was re-designated as a Field Medical Regiment.

UNIFORM AND REGALIA

Dark blue beret with maroon badge backing before being RAO badged. Lanyard thick woven maroon with single strand.

SAF TRANSPORT (SAF TPT)

A HQ MT Transport Platoon was created in 1959 to support the fleet of Land Rovers and Bedford lorries. During 1965 a second platoon was formed in part from men from the donkey platoon. The motor transport was generally known as Force Motor Transport or FMT. A third platoon was raised in 1971, named Dhofar Transport Platoon, which provided support for the Dhofar Governorate. The three platoons combined to form the SAF MT Company including its HQ at BAF. The Armed Forces Motor Transport (AFMT) was created in 1975 due to expansion, this comprised 3 semi-autonomous transport squadrons. The SAFTR Transport Platoon was included in 1978. HQ Transport Squadron was established in MAM in 1980, followed by another platoon. Driver training had been carried out at BAF from 1959 and continued as a Driving School within HQ Sqn FTR from 1980. On 26 March 1980, the Force Transport Regiment (FTR) was formed; all non-unit transport resources and the Army Movements Organization were grouped together under one commanding officer. With an ever-expanding Force Transport Regiment, it was seen prudent to split the regiment into two parts. Consequently, in 1984, the FTR was replaced by 1 Transport Regiment and 2 Transport Regiment. One unit was earmarked for operations and the other for administration work. The service was renamed Sultan's Armed Forces Transport in 1986 and a move from MAM to Seeb also took place that same year. To meet the ever-increasing requirements for the RAO, a School of Transport was created in 1991. A Transport Squadron is provided for Force Medical Services and hundreds of SAF Transport personnel serve with RAO units.

Animal transport had been used within the SAF for many years. There were donkey platoons in some battalions, where they were a unit responsibility and gradually reduced in number after the Dhofar War. Eventually there was one platoon in the north and one platoon in the south, with the southern one disappearing from the order of battle about 1980, and the northern one at JABTC in 1985. Regimental Colours were presented on 10 December 1987 by HM Sultan Qaboos.

UNIFORM AND REGALIA

A dark blue beret is worn. Lanyard woven navy blue/red several strands.

FORCE ORDNANCE SERVICES (FOS)

A SAF Ordnance Section was created in 1961 and enlarged in 1964 to a small Supply Depot at BAF. The depot expanded and was re-designated Force Ordnance Depot (FOD) in 1969. A supply point at Thumrait was established in the late 1960s and known as Ordnance Maintenance Park (OMP), which was renamed 1 OMP in 1971. An Ordnance Maintenance Area was established in Salalah in 1971 and known as 2 OMP. A new depot in MAM Camp was established on 1 September 1973 and later re-designated Base Ordnance Depot and the stores at BAF were moved to that depot. On 26 August 1978, HQ Force Ordnance Depot was relocated to MAM Camp from BAF. With the ebb and flow of the Dhofar War moving westwards the requirement for 1 OMP was diminished and eventually it was disbanded in 1975. The FOS personnel were placed in a Combat Supplies Platoon (C Sups Pl), which was located at Manston (Aydim). This unit was disbanded a year later. At the end of 1976 2 OMP was renamed Forward Ordnance Depot. A Technical Training Wing was established at the Base Ordnance Depot to train clerks and storemen at MAM and eventually became the FOS School. The FOS Barrack Services reorganised into Accommodation Stores Unit for furnishings in all services accommodation. An Ordnance Supply Company was raised to provide first line MT and Technical Spares. FOD Salalah was renamed Ordnance Depot UAG and at the same time a central freight system introduced. A School of Ordnance and Administration opened in 2002.

UNIFORM AND REGALIA

Dark blue beret worn. Lanyard woven blue/red single strand.

ELECTRICAL AND MECHANICAL ENGINEERS (EME)

An EME Workshop for major repairs was formed at BAF in 1957. Prior to this there existed a LAD (Light Aid Detachment) with the MOFF in 1955. Gun Fitters were provided in 1959. An EME School was raised in Bait al Falaj Camp's Fort to train EME personnel, which is now the SAF Museum. The first Force Electrical and Mechanical Engineer (FEME) was appointed in 1962. All infantry battalions had small LADs by 1970. The EME School was established in 1970. In 1972 the first Director EME (DEME) was appointed (Len Mallet REME), and the EME was formally recognised. The main base workshop in Bait al Falaj closed in 1973 when a new workshop was built in Muaskar Al Murtafa (MAM) at Seeb, which is the largest camp in Oman. An EME Training Centre was formed in 1978. Force Medical Equipment Depot was opened in 1983, but because of the technical nature of the work it transferred to EME in 1993. A new EME bio-medical workshop was established in 2003 to support all SAF medical and dental equipment, and the Force Mobile Workshop which was formed in 1984. HQ EME moved to a new building in MAM Camp in 2010. EME has grown over the years to support an expanding Army and has workshops and Light Aid Detachments supporting all major Army units across the country. EME also supports the vehicles used by the Royal Navy of Oman and the Royal Air Force of Oman.

UNIFORM AND REGALIA

EME wear dark blue berets. Lanyard woven single strand blue yellow red.

ROYAL ARMY OF OMAN BAND (RAO BAND)

Both the RAO Band and the RG Bands trace their antecedents to the Pipe Band of Dhofar Force which was raised in the late 1960s. When the Dhofar Force was integrated into the SAF the band became part of the Dhofar Gendarmerie. The band grew and was seen playing at Salalah on occasion. A transfer to the Diwan of Protocol took place in 1973. With the loss of the band a new Pipe Band was raised at Ghallah in 1974 and in the process included some of the original pipers. The requirement was for a Military Band and Corps of Drums along with a Director of Music and additions to the Pipe Band. The band was fully trained and functioning by 1979. A second Pipe Band was created in 1978 and stationed in Salalah as a detached unit under the Pipe Major Instructor. The Pipe Band was relocated to MAM in the mid-1990s to become one large Pipe Band. RAO's School of Music was situated in MAM and a specially built band practice hall was added to the School of Music. There were 250 musicians by the late 1990s. The Band has participated in many Scottish competitions around the world including Brisbane Tattoo and Edinburgh Tattoo. A traditional Omani band has also been formed.

UNIFORM AND REGALIA

The original uniform was a white jacket and black trousers, with black shoes and a black belt. A black Tam o' Shanter and toorie was worn with a red hackle and the instruments were silver. In about 1985, the band changed to red jackets with silver trimmings. Another change took place in 1995 when the trimmings changed to gold, and gold instruments were introduced and the hackle was changed to the Omani colours of white red and green with white being at the top.

UNITS THAT HAVE BEEN DISBANDED
MUSCAT & OMAN FIELD FORCE (MOFF)

Prospecting for oil was the catalyst that created the Muscat & Oman Field Force (MOFF). The International Petroleum Company agreed in 1952 to pay for an armed force to protect the company while prospecting for oil in remote areas of Oman. A British officer and two former Palestine Police men were recruited in 1953 and tasked to build a military force to guard the oil company facilities and convoys. Force training was carried out at Falaj A'Qabail. The Officer Commanding Major P McGill left the force for medical reasons shortly after joining, and Batinah Force officers oversaw the training program until January 1954 when the new Officer Commanding, Lt Colonel Percy Coriat, took charge. He had Major F.W. Haugh and two British captains, George Burton and Alfred Merrell, who were ex-Palestine Police, and two Sudanese officers. A month later, the force known as the Muscat and Oman Field Force consisted of 7 officers and 371 other ranks, although not fully trained. Pressure from the oil company saw an advance company of 125 officers and men, along with IPC staff, being sent to Sawirah Bay adjacent to Duqm. The whole force was in place by March, next to the IPC camp, and shortly after moved to Nafun 15 kilometres up the coast. Training continued and patrols were made with geologists. Reconnaissance into the interior was also carried out in depth. As the force became more competent it was reorganised into the Patrol Squadron (IPC escort), Guard Squadron (camp protection), and Training Group.

The food, conditions and pay were poor and morale consequently suffered. Most of the officers resigned and new ones were recruited. Pay and food were improved and subsequently morale improved by autumn. On 19 October 1954, the MOFF sent an advance party of a troop and 3 Bren gun sections to escort the IPC survey team to Muqbarah, soon to be followed by the

A group of soldiers showing diverse SAF uniforms worn as of 1967. Standing, from left to right: (The unit of the soldier standing on the extreme left at the back is not mentioned. He is in the Oman Gendarmerie which is known as the OG. Please add OG to the caption like this: OG, Guard Company, DR, etc across the line.) Guard Company, DR, FMT, OG, MR, NFR, OIPOG, and Muscat Garrison Guard Company. Front row, from left to right: Coastal Patrol, SOAF, and General Service. (SAF Christmas card by Major-General Corin Purdon, from Muqaddam Ian Buttenshaw Collection)

rest of the expedition. From Muqbarah the expedition moved to Tan'am which was partly deserted. Following a reconnaissance, the town of Ibri surrendered to the MOFF without bloodshed. Lt Col Coriat had planned to depart from the MOFF at the end of 1954 and a new Commanding Officer, Lt Colonel Bill Cheeseman, was flown in during November. The officers under his command were: Maj Haugh, Maj O'Kelly, Capt Barron and Capt Anderson. By the end of 1954 the force strength was 400 men with 5 British officers. The MOFF established a border post at Sunaynah in June 1955. A large consignment of arms for the rebellion was landed near Seeb in the same month but was captured at al-Khawd. Poor pay and bad conditions, particularly at Nafun, caused the soldiers to be very dissatisfied and morale was again very low. After a review of their complaints the Nafun base was closed and better rations provided. In October 1955, the MOFF assisted with the recapture of Buraimi Oasis. This consisted of providing support from Ibri, with a small number of troops to the Trucial Oman Levies who ran the operation. With the success of Buraimi Oasis behind them the Sultan ordered the MOFF to occupy Nizwa which was the capital of the Imamate in the divided country. A column of two rifle squadrons (A and B Sqns), a 3-inch mortar troop, and a composite artillery battery from the Muscat Infantry, comprised of two 3.7-inch guns and two ancient 2.75-inch screw guns, made its way from Ibri to Nizwa. Diplomacy prevailed with the show of force and the Imam fled leaving a few askars and bodyguards to hand over the fort at Nizwa to the MOFF. Pacification and reintegration of the interior to the Sultanate was achieved, but rebels were planning a new invasion in 1956. The MOFF squadron garrisoning Buraimi was replaced by the Muscat Infantry in February and that squadron relocated to Al Qabil in Sharqiyah, less a troop in Fahud. Ibri was the base for a mobile squadron. An artillery troop from the Muscat Infantry was located at Nizwa and a MOFF section at Duqm. Trouble started again in July when MOFF were shot at by rebels and local tribesmen. The force intelligence officer was seriously wounded and two soldiers killed. This was but a foretaste of what was to come in 1957. Force strength in 1956 was a lieutenant colonel, his 2IC, 5 majors, 1 captain, 17 lieutenants, 1 medical officer, 1 quartermaster, 1 MT officer, and 722 rank and file. By the end of the year the MOFF was withdrawn from Sharqiyah and they were re-deployed to Firq as it was regarded as more central. The MOFF comprised of an HQ, HQ Sqn and 3 rifle companies before it became the Oman Regiment. With the reorganisation of the Muscat Armed Forces in 1957, the Muscat and Oman Field Force was re-designated Oman Regiment (OR).

CO Muscat & Oman Field Force trying to establish communications after suffering a major deluge. January 1955. (Courtesy: Muqaddam Ian Buttenshaw)

and white *shemaghs* were also worn in the MOFF by officers. The headdress badge was the standard Army cap badge which depicts the emblem of the Sultan of Oman consisting of a *khunjar*, the Omani dagger, of Al Said family pattern superimposed on crossed *Saifs* (Omani tribal swords). Officer's parade dress was normal tropical khaki dress with Sam Browne belt and khaki peaked cap.

OMAN REGIMENT (OR)

The Muscat and Oman Field Force was re-designated Oman Regiment (OR) with the reorganisation of the Muscat Armed Forces in 1957 and was under the command of Lt Col W Cheeseman. The newly renamed Oman Regiment was deployed to al-Sharqiyah amid the beginnings of a rebellion. Patrols were sent to al-Dhahir but came under accurate medium machine gun fire from trained rebels. However, the rebellion failed on this occasion because the support the rebels expected from Talib bin Ali failed to arrive. This was because Talib's launch ran aground off Ras Tanurah and he had to return with his followers to Saudi Arabia. By mid-June

UNIFORM AND REGALIA

The Muscat & Oman Field Force wore the regular Muscat Armed Forces khaki uniform. They were issued with red hose tops and brick red *shemaghs* worn like a turban. Photographic evidence records that red

Muscat and Oman Field Force on Parade at Ibri December 1954. Note red *shemagh* worn as a turban. (Courtesy: Muqaddam Ian Buttenshaw)

the regiment had returned to its camp at Raddah, near Firq. About this time another group of rebels landed at Khawr Diyan, on the al-Batinah coast, with arms and several hundred followers. The MAF forces were only four companies strong including the OR company from Buraimi. A Company of the OR was ordered to capture Bilad Sayt and destroy it, thus forcing the tribe there to disassociate itself from the rebels. The company was held up by rebel fire during the attack and while waiting for artillery support from mountain guns before continuing the attack, rebels started ambushing and mining the lines of communication. The regiment required assistance, and reinforcements consisting of a company of the Muscat Regiment, and the mountain guns, were sent from Sohar via Ibri. Rebel support increased and an OR vehicle carrying wounded men was ambushed and the wounded were killed. With the worsening situation the Commanding Officer abandoned the Bilad Sayt operation and made a tactical withdrawal. While retiring, the OR were ambushed at Tanuf, Kamah and Nizwa al Ulayah and the withdrawal became a rout with vehicles and stores abandoned and the OR retired to Raddah and Fahud. The detachment in Nizwa fort was left behind and surrendered to rebels. About half of the regiment deserted, with the exception of a company at Buraimi. Those that remained were flown to Sohar. The regiment had been effectively destroyed and Lt Col Cheeseman was dismissed from the MAF by the Sultan. The remainder of the regiment was absorbed into other units.

UNIFORM AND REGALIA

The working uniform and badges remained the same as the Muscat and Oman Field Force and the red headdress probably remained for ceremonial guards.

DHOFAR FORCE (DF)

The Dhofar Force was an independent unit which reported directly to the Sultan and was not a part of the MAF and not absorbed into the SAF until 1970. Dhofar Force was raised in 1955 by Major St John Armitage who was earlier 2IC of Batinah Force. Major Armitage was authorized by the Sultan to be sent to Salalah to raise this small force, which was to be based at Arzat, close to Salalah, and had section bases around Dhofar and into the desert. Small garrisons

were maintained at Taqah, Mirbat, Ayn Arzat, Ayn Sahalnawt, Mughsin and Shisr. The force was comprised initially of about 50 Baluch soldiers who were tasked with manning several garrisons. Eventually, local Dhofar tribesmen, or Jebali, were recruited into the force along with men from Salalah with African origins, sometimes known as the *khaddam*, who had formerly been slaves. The unit also provided men for ceremonial duties and guarding the perimeters of the Sultan's palaces. Major St John Armitage left the DF in 1959, being succeeded by Lt Col Eric Johnson. While inspecting the Dhofar Force at Razat camp in April 1966, Sultan Said suffered an assassination attempt when two of the soldiers in the ceremonial guard tried to shoot him at close range but missed. There were, however, some casualties amongst the Dhofar Force and the Sultan's entourage; Lt Col Mohammed Sakhi Raja, a Pakistani, Commander of Dhofar Force, was severely wounded, and 2Lt Sattar Shah died of wounds. The force was subsequently disarmed by the NFR. Twenty-two Arab soldiers were imprisoned and 19 deserted, however the *khaddam* remained loyal. As a consequence of the action the force was purged and was left mainly with *khaddam* soldiers who proved to be more reliable than the local Jebali. The unit was reorganised but was not particularly effective. After the coup in 1970 Sultan Qaboos re-designated the force as the Dhofar Gendarmerie within the SAF and with superior manpower and all the benefits of the SAF.

UNIFORM AND REGALIA

Khaki uniform and dark brown beret worn.

DHOFAR GENDARMERIE (DG)

When the Dhofar Force, which had always been an independent military force answerable directly to the Sultan, was taken into the SAF in 1970 it was re-designated as the Dhofar Gendarmerie. Initially recruited from Dhofari and Baluch, the Dhofari were phased out and Baluch recruited to replace them. The *khaddam* were also phased out and went into the UAG Garrison Guard. The unit came under the command of the resident Salalah Plain battalion where their tasks included providing security but this was delayed due to initial poor recruitment. Wherever they were located they were also charged with clearing the roads and airfields within their area of responsibility and some combat companies worked with Firqat. Eventually the gendarmerie reached 400 men, which enabled them to have eight troops, whilst two troops from the Oman Gendarmerie were also loaned to them.

With the manning problems of 1971 the DG were obliged to withdraw one of the 3 sections at Mirbat and Taqah. In 1972, the DG manned Habrut Fort with a troop, along with a group of Firqat and BATT instructors, on the Yemen border. They came under heavy fire from a company of PDRY soldiers armed with machine guns, rifles and mortars who were stationed in the fort opposite the Omani

Dhofar Gendarmerie guard of honour marching into position at Salalah airport. They are all wearing the burnt-orange hackle on their berets. (Muqaddam Ian Buttenshaw Collection)

The FV601 Saladin six-wheeled armoured car was made by the British company Alvis. Its primary armament was the 76mm L5A1 gun. This vehicle is shown in typical colours for the Omani armed forces, which initially operated eight Saladins in the Armoured Car Squadron in 1971. More were obtained later. The type was subsequently replaced by the Scorpion light tank. (Artwork by David Bocquelet)

A Panhard *Vehicule Blinde Leger* (VBL, light armoured vehicle) with a launcher for a BGM-71 TOW anti-tank guided missile and a MAG GPMG. Oman acquired more than 130 VBLs over the last 20 years, and all of which are camouflaged in sand and olive green. (Artwork by David Bocquelet)

The Alvis FV101 Scorpion was a British-made armoured reconnaissance vehicle with primary armament consisting of the 76mm L23A1 gun and a co-axial 7.62mm L43A1 machine gun. Thirty-seven FV101 Scorpions were acquired by Oman between late 1982 and late 1983, together with three FV106 Samson armoured recovery vehicles. Another batch was delivered in 1985, this time including 31 FV105 Sultan, 34 FV103 Spartan and 27 FV106 Samson vehicles. (Artwork by David Bocquelet)

The M60A3 main battle tanks are operated by the Type 59 Regiment. This unit consists of three squadrons, each with 19 tanks, plus two in the HQ section. Main armament of the type is the 105mm M68 gun, based on the British Royal Ordnance L7. (Artwork by David Bocquelet)

The Vickers Defence Systems FV4034 Challenger 2 is a British Main Battle Tank, which represents the heaviest combat vehicle of the Omani armed forces. The type is operated by the Type 38 Regiment, which consists of two squadrons, each with 19 tanks. Primary armament consists of the 120mm L30A1 rifled gun with 50 rounds. (Artwork by David Bocquelet)

The MOWAG Piranha II is a Swiss-made wheeled armoured personnel carrier, of which Oman acquired a total of 174 vehicles, including turreted, mortar, APC, command post, observation post, recovery and ambulance versions. This example is one of the standard APCs, capable of carrying 16 troops and equipped with a 12.7mm machine gun in a locally-made turret. (Artwork by David Bocquelet)

The first 'combat' aircraft of the SOAF were armed Provost T.Mk 52 trainers flown by RAF contract pilots. They were operated by what subsequently became No. 1 Squadron from Salalah AB. All Omani Provosts wore a standard camouflage pattern in dark sea grey (BS381C/638, FS36173) and dark green (BS381C/641, FS34079) over, with undersides in high speed silver finish. Original national insignia consisted of the white shield (outlined with red) with an early version of the Sultanate's crest in red on the fin, and roundels in red (outlined in white), with the crest in white, applied on top and bottom surfaces of the wing. Known serials were WV678 and XF907. Their armament consisted of 25-pounder bombs (four per wing) and 3-in HVAR unguided rockets (two per wing). (Artwork by Tom Cooper)

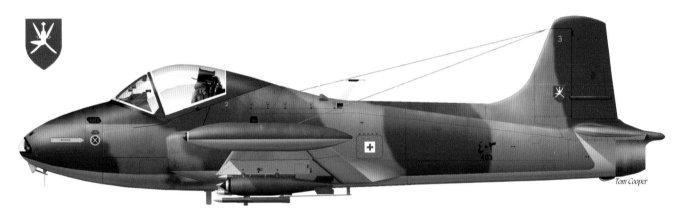

By 1971-1972, the SOAF operated a full squadron of Strikemaster light attack aircraft. All were camouflaged in dark green (BS381C/641) and dark earth (BS381C/350) or mid stone (BS381C/362) on top surfaces and sides, and light aircraft grey (BS381C/627) on undersurfaces. National markings meanwhile consisted of the crest of the Sultanate in white applied on a red shield, on the fin, and large roundels in red and white on top and bottom wing surfaces. Serials (401-425) were applied in black on the rear fuselage, in Farsi digits atop of Arabic digits: the last digit was repeated in orange on the top of either side of the fin. Usual armament consisted of two banks of Hispano Suiza Sura unguided rockets and a single 250-pound bomb under each wing. (Artwork by Tom Cooper)

The third crucial type in service with the SOAF of the early 1970s was the Agusta-Bell AB.205 Huey utility helicopter – all donated by Iran. Photographs from the mid-1970s usually show them equipped with a Search and Rescue winch (SAR-winch) installed atop the right side of the cockpit and wearing a wrap-around camouflage in dark earth (BS381C/350) and dark green (BS381C/641). Serials (701-725) were applied in Farsi atop of Arabic digits, in black, on the boom in front of the horizontal stabilizer. Operated by No. 3 Squadron, they saw extensive service in support of the SAS and local firqat during the campaigns to secure the areas in Dhofar along the coast east of Salalah. (Artwork by Tom Cooper)

The SOAF received its first three Shorts SC.Mk 3 Skyvan (Skyvan 3M) light transports in 1971. Subsequent acquisition of 13 additional examples enabled the establishment of the original No. 2 Squadron. The availability of such a large number of STOL light transports enabled the SAF to move troops and supplies to multiple rugged, often primitive landing strips, only a few hundred yards long, and close to the combat zone. As usual, all have received a wrap-around camouflage pattern in dark earth (BS381C/350) and dark green (BS381C/641). Through the mid-1970s, the section of roof atop the cockpit was often painted in white to decrease the effects of the sun. Serials (901-916) were applied in Persian atop of Arabic digits, in black, on the rear fuselage. (Artwork by Tom Cooper)

By far the most potent strike aircraft of the Dhofar War were McDonnell Douglas F-4D and F-4E Phantom II fighter-bombers of the IIAF. Detachments of between 4 and 10 aircraft were usually deployed at Bait al Falaj and/or Masirah ABs from late 1972. All wore the standardised camouflage pattern called 'Asia Minor' in yellow sand (FS30400), dark earth (FS30140) and dark green (FS34079) on top surfaces and sides, and light grey (FS36622) on undersurfaces. Prior to January 1976, they wore serials consisting of four digits, including a prefix 3 (for 'combat aircraft') and the aircraft's individual serial. This example was one of the first 32 F-4Es acquired by Iran: serial number 3-655 (US FY-number 69-7732), from 11th TFS, home-based at 'Tactical Fighter Base 1' at Mehrabad, Tehran (as indicated by the black 1 inside a black circle applied below the fin flash). Usual armament consisted of 6-12 Mk.82 or 6-11 M117 general-purpose bombs. CBU-58s were deployed occasionally but most of the time Iranian Phantoms used only their 20mm M61A1 Vulcan cannons in combat. (Artwork by Tom Cooper)

The IIAA originally deployed a mix of 32 AB.205 Huey general purpose helicopters and AB.206 JetRanger scout helicopters to Oman, starting from late 1972. Essentially equipped in exactly the same fashion as the AB.205s donated to the SOAF, they often wore a mix of Iranian and SOAF markings, including (from front towards the rear) the official crest of the IIAA (on the cockpit doors), service title (on cabin doors), SOAF and the Iranian roundel, and an Omani fin-flash (in place of the IIAA serial). Their original camouflage pattern consisted of beige and light brown on top surfaces and sides, and light grey on undersurfaces. (Artwork by Tom Cooper)

Agusta-Bell/Bell Model 206 JetRanger – a total of 214 of which were acquired by Tehran during the early 1970s – was the principal scout helicopter of the Imperial Iranian Battle Group in Oman. As far as is known, they were camouflaged in similar colours to those applied on AB.205s of the IIAA but retained Iranian national markings. Known serials of examples in service with the IIAA as of 1972-1976 were in the range 4-701 – 4-758. As illustrated in this artwork, several were modified to carry the Emerson mini-TAT installation including the M134 Minigun 7.62mm six-barrel rotary machine gun, on a sponson below the fuselage (fed by a chain-link from an ammunition box inside the rear cabin). (Artwork by Tom Cooper)

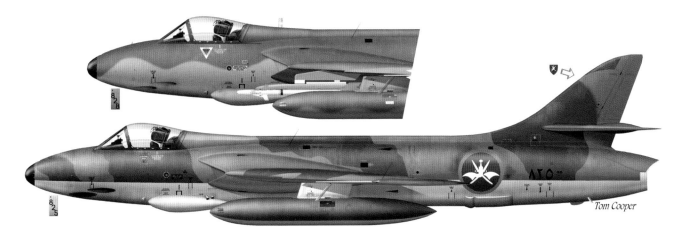

Starting in early 1975, Jordan donated a total of 31 Hunters to Oman. Used to form No. 5 Squadron, these included a mix of FGA.Mk 73A/B fighter-bombers, FR.Mk 10 reconnaissance fighters, and two T.Mk 66 two-seat conversion trainers. Initially upon delivery, all wore the standard – even though heavily worn out – camouflage pattern in dark sea grey (BS381C/638, FS36173) and dark green (BS381C/641, FS34079) over, with undersides in high speed silver finish. During the mid-1980s, surviving examples were overhauled and re-painted in two variants of a camouflage pattern consisting of ghost grey (FS36320) and dark ghost grey (FS35237): while dark ghost gray was usually applied along the same pattern as the dark green of earlier times, at least the FGA.Mk 73 serial number 825 (shown in upper inset) received this colour applied along all of its top surfaces instead. Notable is that by this time many of SOAF's Hunters were modified to carry AIM-9P Sidewinder air-to-air missiles. (Artwork by Tom Cooper)

Several of the AB.205s overhauled in the 1980s and 1990s received a new camouflage pattern consisting of light stone (BS381C/361) and dark brown (BS381C/411) on upper surfaces and sides, and light grey on undersurfaces. Serials remained small and were still applied in a similar fashion to usual, in black with Farsi digits atop those in Arabic. Notable is the addition of the exhaust diffuser, which led engine exhausts directly into the propeller downwash, and armour plates on the sides of the engine housing: a measure introduced to decrease the helicopter's vulnerability to small-arms fire and SA-7 MANPADs. (Artwork by Tom Cooper)

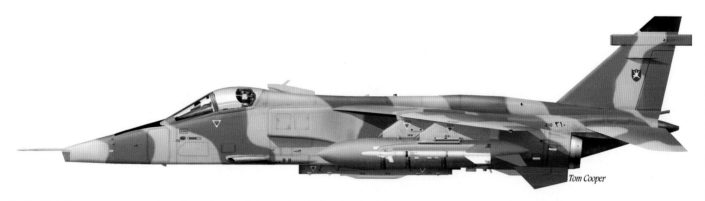

The SEPECAT Jaguar International serial number 210 belonged to the first batch of this type acquired in 1977 and 1978 and assigned to No. 1 Squadron SOAF. All were painted in a standardized, wrap-around camouflage pattern consisting of light stone (BS381C/361) and dark earth (BS381C/350). Although originally acquired as fighter-bombers, Omani Jaguars were modified to carry AIM-9P Sidewinder air-to-air missiles on their outboard underwing hardpoints because of having a secondary air defence role. The second batch of Jaguars included the provision to carry French-made Matra R.550 Magic air-to-air missiles on underwing pylons too. (Artwork by Tom Cooper)

The BAE Systems Hawk T.Mk 103 is a two-seat advanced weapons trainer with a HOTAS-cockpit and additional avionics, including the forward-looking infra-red system and a laser ranger installed in an extended nose. Other equipment includes the BAE Sky Guardian radar-warning-receiver and wing-tip rails for AIM-9 Sidewinder air-to-air missiles. Oman acquired a total of four, delivered between December 1993 and January 1994: the rest of the same order consisted of 15 Hawk 203s, while eight much more advanced Hawk T.Mk 166 were acquired from 2017. In service with the RAFO, Hawks are used as lead-in trainers for more potent types – including F-16s and EF-2000s. (Artwork by Tom Cooper)

Oman signed a contract for an order for 12 F-16C/D Block 50s in May 2002 (in the Peace A'sama A'safiya II programme), and the first example – the two-seater F-16D shown here – was accepted on 19 July 2005. A follow-up order for 10 F-16Cs and 2 F-16Ds was signed in December 2011. All are powered by General Electric F110-GE-129 engines, equipped with AN/APG-68(V)XM radars, and compatible with a total of 14 SNIPER and 7 PANTERA targeting pods with terrain following radars – making them some of the most powerful F-16s to ever enter service. Moreover, the RAFO acquired a total of 50 AIM-120C ARMAAM and 100 AIM-9X Sidewinder air-to-air missiles, a wide range of guided air-to-ground and air-to-surface missiles, and Goodrich DB-110 airborne reconnaissance systems for them. All aircraft are painted in a 50:50 mix of grays FS36622 and FS35237, and wear the usual three-digit serials (801-825) in Arabic and Persian digits on the rear fuselage. (Artwork by Tom Cooper)

Female Lieutenant Colonel – Royal Oman Police

Women of the ROP serve more commonly as traffic police or in administrative and logistical functions, but they are gradually gaining higher ranks and greater responsibility. The training is rigorous and in recent times they have achieved functions and positions previously occupied only by men. The ROP also has an all women music band. The female police uniform has been adapted to Muslim traditions and incorporates a feminine version of the service cap. Also shown is the ROP emblem.

Infantry Soldier – Royal Army of Oman

The soldier wears RAO camouflage kit which is unique to the Army. His headdress is the *shemagh* and it is worn bound around the head turban style. Webbing is the British Personal Load Carrying Equipment (PLCE) while the boots are designed for desert use. His weapon is a Steyr AUG A3 5.56 × 45mm NATO assault rifle, manufactured in Austria by Steyr Mannlicher GmbH & Co KG. The RAO emblem is also depicted.

Guard Commander – Muscat Garrison

Muscat Garrison Guard Company (MUSGAR). The Staff Sergeant is armed with a Short Magazine Lee-Enfield Rifle Mk III. Wearing a tropical khaki drill shirt and shorts along with a red sash, he proudly wears his 1958/9 Jebel Akhdar (Green Mountain) Campaign Medal (diagonal narrow stripes dark green & red ribbon) followed by a Long Service & Good Conduct medal (plain red ribbon). He has a traditional Oman headdress known as *qulla* or *kumma*. This khaki hat was first worn in the SAF by the Muscat Regiment. The woollen *agal* is red unlike the *agal* for the Muscat Regiment which was yellow and red. When Sultan Qaboos superseded his father as Sultan in 1970 he ordered the *qulla* be replaced with a scarlet beret. Brown Muscat sandals are worn with red hosetops and short khaki puttees. His belt is a British 1937 pattern white blancoed web belt with brass fittings.

Royal Guard of Oman

The guardsman is wearing black ceremonial dress with gold piping and has the distinctive RGO maroon beret as maroon is the official colour of the RGO. A white belt is worn with a chrome buckle on which the emblem of the RGO is superimposed. A gold aguillette is worn on the right shoulder. He is armed with an assault rifle, the 5.56mm M16A2, which is the preferred ceremonial and drill firearm of all the Sultan's armed forces. The maroon banner depicts the emblem of the Royal Guard and the scrolls read: Sultan of Oman, Dhofar, Sultan of Oman's Guard Company.

A pair of SOAF SEPECAT Jaguar strike aircraft. The British-French jet attack aircraft was used in the close air support role and as a fighter bomber. (Muqaddam Ian Buttenshaw Collection)

SOAF Short Skyvan on landing. British made 19-seat twin-turboprop aircraft. (Muqaddam Ian Buttenshaw Collection)

A C-130 Hercules four-engine turboprop military transport aircraft. (Muqaddam Ian Buttenshaw Collection)

Pair of BAE Systems Hawk signal engine jet aircraft of SOAF. (Muqaddam Ian Buttenshaw Collection)

Dakota used for troop transport from Northern Oman to Dhofar in the 1970s. (Muqaddam Ian Buttenshaw Collection)

RAFO AgustaWestland Super Lynx 300 firing unguided rockets while training. (Courtesy: Muqaddam Ian Buttenshaw)

RAFO Pipe Band inspected by H.M. Sultan Qaboos Bin Said. (Muqaddam Ian Buttenshaw Collection)

RAFO Pipe Band at practise, all wearing RAFO camouflage kit. (Muqaddam Ian Buttenshaw Collection)

Male and female drummers of the RAFO Band. Note the silver wire wove trade badge depicting a drum on a yellow cloth background. (Muqaddam Ian Buttenshaw Collection)

RNO Officer on the bridge during routine patrol wearing work rig. (Muqaddam Ian Buttenshaw Collection)

Nasr al-Bahr, an early Omani military dhow. (Muqaddam Ian Buttenshaw Collection)

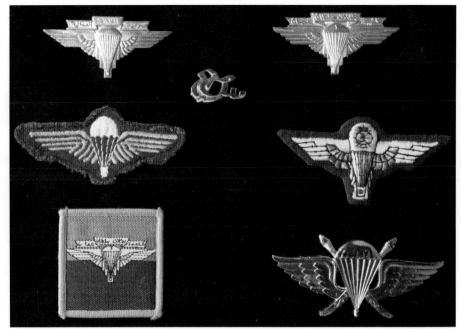

Parachute Unit badges and insignia (from left to right): Para Squadron, Para Regiment (with 1 on the canopy), shoulder title cloth wings, and cloth arm patch. (Eddie Parks Collection)

Top: SSF badges and insignia. Officer's wire wove headdress badge. Second row: shoulder wings, lilac OR's beret badge and officer's wings. Bottom row: gold shoulder title and metal OR's cap badge with mess dress collar badges. (Eddie Parks Collection)

Officers embroidered breast badge 1 Parachute Regiment. (Eddie Parks Collection)

RGO in ceremonial dress while inspected by HM Sultan Qaboos. (Muqaddam Ian Buttenshaw Collection)

RGO 3 Squadron Royal Guard, Mounted Pipes Band. (Pipe Major Gavin Moffat)

Sultan's Special Forces on parade with their standard. Note the force's colour, which is lilac, and their distinctive camouflage kit. (Muqaddam Ian Buttenshaw Collection)

Sultan's Special Forces officers receiving Sultan's Commendation Medal which has a plain blue ribbon and sometimes bears a leaf device for more specific action/service. SSF black with gold motif circular cloth unit patch on left shoulder. Wire wove beret badge. Post 2000. (Courtesy: Muqaddam Ian Buttenshaw)

Officer's beret 3 Regt Border Guard Brigade. (Muqaddam Ian Buttenshaw Collection)

RAO SHOULDER BADGES

HEADQUARTERS

HQ RAO

11 INF BDE

23 INF BDE

BDR GD
BDE

HQ MS

HQ FQ

INFANTRY

MR

NFR

DR

JR

OCR

FF

KJ

WFR

SO PARA

ORR

WBSF

CSF

MSF

ARMS/SERVICES

MSO

SOA

SAFE

SAF Sigs

FMS

SAF Tpt

FOS

EME

OTHER UNITS

SAFTR

RAO BAND

GAR
MAM

GAR
SAL

Cloth shoulder patches worn by the SAF. (Muqaddam Ian Buttenshaw Collection)

Captain Berty Bowes from the Muscat Regiment, in the early 1960s. Note the brass MR shoulder title and the red and white checked *shemagh* with *agal*, which was worn by the Muscat Regiment and the SAF headdress badge. (Major E. Parks Collection)

Dhofar Force Recruit late 1950s. (Muqaddam Ian Buttenshaw Collection)

RAO Guard of Honour outside HQ RAO. (Muqaddam Ian Buttenshaw Collection)

A Bugler and a Guard Commander of the MUSGAR Guard Company, on 21 Jul 1970 – probably the last time the *qulla* or *kumma* hat was worn: they were replaced by red berets on insistence of Sultan Qaboos, two days later. (Muqaddam Ian Buttenshaw Collection)

The parade commander from OG on the first National Day parade. (Muqaddam Ian Buttenshaw Collection)

NFR LMG-gunner in Dhofar of 1969. Note his self-painted camouflage fatigues. (Muqaddam Ian Buttenshaw Collection)

VBL reconnaissance vehicle with TOW 2 and a MAG 7.62 GPMG. The TAC sign is that of the Parachute Regiment. (Muqaddam Ian Buttenshaw Collection

Oerlikon GDF-007 twin 35mm cannon, normally deployed in pairs with a generator and C&C radar. (Muqaddam Ian Buttenshaw Collection)

A Panhard Véhicule Blindé Léger or light armoured vehicle armed with a M2 12.7mm Browning HMG. The sand coloured square TAC sign denotes the VBL belongs to the Desert Regiment. (Muqaddam Ian Buttenshaw Collection)

Mowag Piranha II – the so called 'Desert Piranha', in its mortar variant (Oman acquired seven variants) with the L16A1 81mm ROF Mortar. (Muqaddam Ian Buttenshaw Collection)

Challenger 2 MBT at speed during training. (Muqaddam Ian Buttenshaw Collection)

M60A3 MBT. The M60s form a Type 59 Regiment with three squadrons of 19 tanks and two in its HQ. (Muqaddam Ian Buttenshaw Collection)

Scorpion light tank with 76mm gun. Designed as an armoured reconnaissance vehicle, the tank was air portable. (Muqaddam Ian Buttenshaw Collection)

A South African-made ARMSCOR G6 self-propelled 155mm howitzer, of which sixty-four have been purchased. (Muqaddam Ian Buttenshaw Collection)

A Toyota ¾ ton Desert Patrol general purpose vehicle with a roll bar, seen while firing a TOW ATGM. (Muqaddam Ian Buttenshaw Collection)

Alvis Saladin armoured car, which was replaced by the Scorpion light tank. It was highly regarded in desert conditions and had a crew of three. (Muqaddam Ian Buttenshaw Collection)

Toyota 3/4 ton Desert Patrol vehicle with roll bar. The TAC Sign is ORR. The vehicle is armed with a 7.62mm GPMG (MAG). Note the camouflage, as the ORR operate in the desert it has two shades of brown and is the only unit in RAO with these colours. (Muqaddam Ian Buttenshaw Collection)

This Toyota ¾ ton Desert Patrol vehicle with a roll bar is either from the CSF or the WBSF. It is equipped with the GPMG on the front and a .50 Cal Browning HMG in the back. (Muqaddam Ian Buttenshaw Collection)

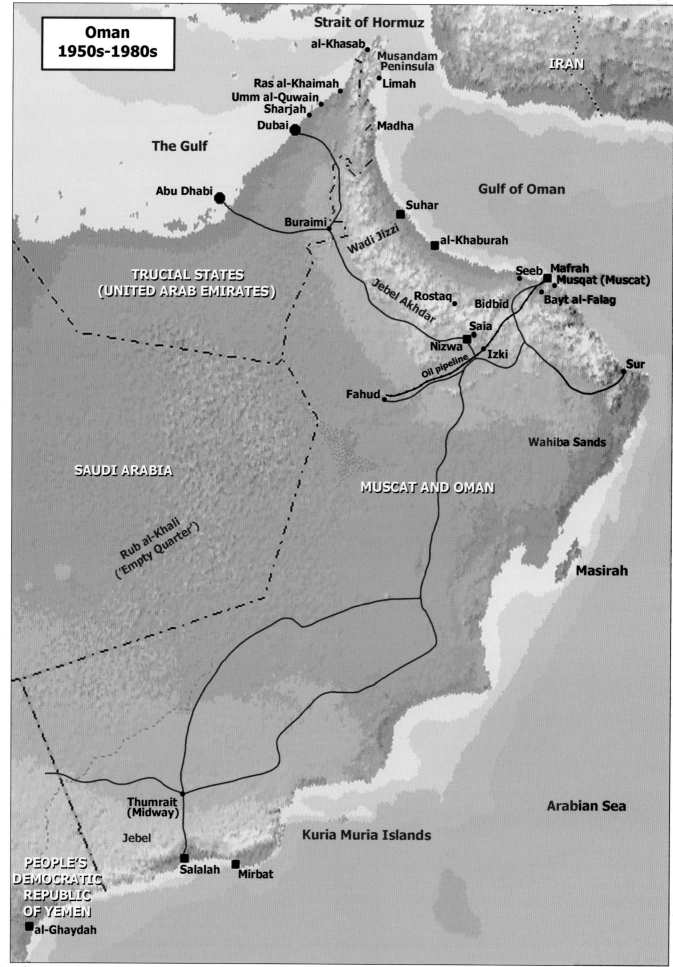

Map of Muscat and Oman and surrounding countries as in the 1950s – 1980s period. (Map by Tom Cooper)

fort. Air strikes were called in and the DG were exfiltrated. A series of heavy airstrikes by SOAF followed destroying supplies and locations inside the Yemen border. The troop at Habrut was relocated to Mirbat and was unfortunate to come under attack by guerrilla forces, 200-250 strong, of hard-core foreign trained fighters. Whilst *en route* to Mirbat these foreign fighters killed the members of the DG picket on the Jebel Ali but in doing so alerted a second picket who managed an escape to a prepared position on the beach. The shooting alerted Mirbat and the forces there were able to prepare for the attack. The DG was eventually disbanded and the Jebalis moved to the Firqats, while the Dhofaris transferred to the SAF units particularly the KJ, the Royal Guard and Dhofar Independent Company.

Changing the guard at Muscat Palace, on 15 September 1970, as OG were taking over from the (all-Baluch) MUSGAR Guard Company. The departing Guard Company is seen wearing their new red berets instead of the *kummas*. (Muqaddam Ian Buttenshaw)

UNIFORM AND REGALIA

Similar to Oman Gendarmerie, but with a bottle green beret and a burnt orange hackle and backing behind the cap badge for parades. The hackle was discontinued when they were absorbed into the KJ, but the badge backing was retained.

DHOFAR GUARD UNIT (DGU)

The DGU was raised in 1975 and deployed a company at Thumrait (Midway) located near an old oil camp. Thumrait acted as a resupply depot and a staging point for regiments to redeploy. DGU were not a first line regiment but more of a static guard unit, which also provided a guard company at Aydim (Manston). After the conclusion of the war in 1976, the DGU no longer had a purpose and along with the remnants of Z Company formed another Baluch unit, the new Western Frontier Regiment.

INDEPENDENT GUARD UNIT (IGU)

The Independent Guard Unit was raised at BAF in 1960 and was also involved with the expansion of existing units. In 1961 they became re-designated as the Muscat Garrison Guard Unit.

UNIFORM AND REGALIA

Headdress was the khaki *qulla* skull cap with red and yellow woollen *agal*. The uniform was from the MR.

MUSCAT GARRISON GUARD COMPANY (MUSGAR)

A professional military garrison was first provided by Indian Army troops stationed in Muscat in 1913. They were followed by the Muscat Levy Corps, the Muscat Infantry and Muscat Regiment. The Muscat Infantry was little more than a garrison guard for Muscat, providing troops for vital points in the capital. After re-designation in 1957 to the Muscat Regiment, as a fully-fledged infantry battalion, its garrison duties were transferred to the newly raised Independent Guard Unit in 1960. The name was changed in 1961 to Muscat Garrison (MUSGAR) Independent Guard Company. MUSGAR provided a garrison force of two platoons in Muscat based at Fort Mirani and provided guards for the palace, Bait al Barza adjacent to the palace, and the British Consulate General. Another detachment guarded the prisoners at Fort Jalali. The British Consulate General guard was discontinued in 1968 after 56 years of duty. A small detachment from MUSGAR was deployed to Mugshin in the Dhofari Nejd in the 1960s taking over from Dhofar Force. In 1970, the Oman Gendarmerie Palace Sector (PALSEC) took over garrison duties from MUSGAR, which was later renamed F Sqn OG, which in turn became the Royal Guard Sqn in 1973. F Sqn was then removed from OG Order of Battle.

MUSGAR Guard Company expanded to 3 small companies: X, Y, and Z. Z Company was permanently detached to Dhofar in 1969, and X and Y Companies remained in BAF. When the SAF moved to the larger military camp at Rusayle in 1973, the unit became known as the Muaskar al Mutafa'aa (MAM) Garrison Guard. The MAM Garrison provided facilities for the regiments and services and also included a Tri-Service Headquarters. The remnants in BAF became known as the BAF Garrison Guard.

During the War in Dhofar there was a requirement for a garrison in Salalah and Thumrait (Midway). The Baluch Z Independent Company of MUSGAR was stationed in Salalah in the latter part of 1969. This company was a mobile unit that patrolled the Salalah Plains and used Land Rovers armed with .50 Browning Machine Guns and also carried out reconnaissance and daily mine clearing. Thumrait was taken over by the SAF from the Oil Company in 1972 and made into a garrison (THUMGAR), which was tasked to control operations on the north side of Jebel Dhofar. There was already a military presence at Thumrait as troops from MUSGAR had been there since 1968 to assist as a staging and re-supply point by forces moving north, south and operating in the Nejd.

With the paucity of Vickers Machine Guns in the SAF they were all retained by the MUSGAR MMG Platoon who then loaned out detachments when required to whatever regiment had a need for them in Dhofar.

UNIFORM AND REGALIA

Before 1970 MUSGAR wore the khaki *qulla* style hats with a woollen red *agal*. Sultan Qaboos ordered the *qulla* be replaced by a ceremonial scarlet beret from 1970. Parade dress was khaki shirts and shorts, *chaplis*, without socks, puttees and red hose tops. The MAM Garrison wore a red beret and the lanyard was thick green/red woven two strand.

NORTHERN OMAN BORDER SCOUTS (NOBS)

The Northern Oman Border Scouts was formed on 1 July 1974. Established in northern Oman, the role was to patrol and maintain surveillance over the land and sea borders of the Sultanate to deter and prevent illegal immigration, gun running, smuggling and effectively relieve the OG from manning some of the smaller border posts. However, the Scouts were under the administrative control of the OG, which also did the initial training. NOBS consisted of HQ and Troops at Qabil (Western Sector), Khatmat Milahah (Northern Sector), Suwaiq (Central Sector), and Balad Bani bu Ali (Southern Sector). There were also Troops at Sumaini and Aswad in the Ibri area. A Training Troop was located at Hazm. With the end of the war in Dhofar, the whole unit was transferred to the Royal Oman Police on 1 July 1976.

UNIFORM AND REGALIA

NOBS wore the same uniform as the Oman Gendarmerie and had a red and white *shemagh* but no lanyard.

PENINSULA REINFORCEMENT BATTALION (PRB)

The Peninsular Reinforcement Battalion was one of the northern based battalions, which was nominated PRB for a year. A company, which changed every 4 months, would be sent to Musandam while the rest of the battalion was available to reinforce the area by sea and air if required. There were also four 130mm guns left in Khassab, with a two-man maintenance crew, and gunners could be flown in if required. Reinforcement exercises named Lamaát Al Barq took place in early 1982 and 1985. In 1981, the PRB also deployed sections of 81mm mortars and GPMG (SF) to defend both SON's RAS Musandam base and Little Quoin Island because of the threat

Royal Guard Band plaid brooch. (Cliff Lord Collection)

Royal Guard headdress badge and shoulder title. (Cliff Lord Collection)

Royal Guard of Oman headdress badge. (Cliff Lord Collection)

to the Strait of Hormuz during the Iran-Iraq War. The presence of actual PRB troops were phased out in the late 1980s, except for the mortars and GPMG sections, until eventually those responsibilities were handed over to the new Naval Security Unit in the early 1990s. A battalion remained as PRB until 2003, when the MSF was further increased in size.

3
ROYAL GUARD OF OMAN (RGO)

With the accession of Sultan Qaboos as ruler of Oman it was deemed necessary that he should have a bodyguard. In the short term this matter was resolved by the British Army Training Team from the SAS providing the initial bodyguard and training a permanent Omani bodyguard. The Baluch Muscat Garrison Guard Company, being entirely Baluch, was considered to be inappropriate to guard the Sultan's palaces. Consequently, three new OG troops were transferred as OG Palace Sector (PALSEC). Two troops were sent for training with the BATT and the third was based at Fort Mirani where they were charged with guarding the old palace in Muscat and manned a saluting battery at the fort. By April 1972 the bodyguard was an independent unit of the OG with command and control by the SAF until 1973 when it became the Royal Guard Squadron, but with an Oman Gendarmerie officer in command. Expansion occurred and the unit was re-designated Royal Guard

Badge of the Oman Mounted Band. (Cliff Lord Collection)

Office of the Sultan, badge. (Cliff Lord Collection)

Oman Royal Stables Badge. (Cliff Lord Collection)

Oman Royal Stables Patch. (Cliff Lord Collection)

Regiment in May 1975 and Regimental Colours were presented that November.

During 1981 the regiment was reorganised into a brigade, and on 1 November 1983 HM the Sultan presented his personal Royal Standard to the Royal Guard Brigade and this date is now considered the Royal Guard Day. With continuous expansion and development, the Royal Guard Brigade was to become a large integrated combat formation. Re-designation of the Royal Guard of Oman occurred in June 1987, as a separate military force from the RAO. The Royal

Household was added to the Royal Guard of Oman later in the year. Very high standards of military training were expected, and modern equipment was procured along with sophisticated weapon systems. The RGO is a Light Infantry Brigade but also provides personal security for the Sultan and Royal Family. The Motorcycle VIP Convoy Escort have a display team called the Red Helmets, and there is a Parachute Team. Further to this there is also the Oman Royal Yacht Squadron and the Royal Flight of Oman. The RGO is headquartered at al-Aman Barracks in Seeb. An overview of the Sultan's Forces Royal Guard of Oman is given in Table 21.

Table 21: Sultan's Forces Royal Guard of Oman
Element
Royal Guard Brigade
1 Guard Regiment
2 Guard Regiment
Royal Guard Armoured Squadron
Royal Guard Bands
Royal Guard of Oman School of Technology

Swiss GAI-DO1 twin anti-aircraft guns. The two in the foreground are mounted on what appear to be French ACMAT VLRA 6x6, with the rear two on French VAB 6x6 AFVs, a small number of which were specifically purchased to mount these weapons in support of the armoured brigade. (Muqaddam Ian Buttenshaw Collection)

VAB AFV in 6x6 configuration. The triple missile mount is a Shorts Missile Systems, Belfast (now Thales Air Defence), Lightweight Multiple Launcher (LML), with Javelin short range MANPADS (man-portable air-defence system). (Muqaddam Ian Buttenshaw Collection)

ROYAL HOUSEHOLD, UNIFORM AND REGALIA

The Royal Guard wear a maroon beret, and a maroon stable belt. Combat kit is the old British DPM pattern.

ROYAL GUARD BOYS TECHNICAL SCHOOL & ROYAL GUARD OF OMAN SCHOOL OF TECHNOLOGY

The Royal Guard Boys Technical School was established in 1976. Extra to the regular school subjects, emphasis was placed on practical technical expertise. The Royal Guard Boys Technical School was re-designated as the Royal Guard of Oman School of Technology in March 1988.

ROYAL BAND

During 1984 training began for a Royal Guard symphony orchestra. Bands were required for the ceremonial aspect of the role. The Royal Band became the Royal Band (South) at Salalah, which was followed by the Royal Band (North) at Seeb. Another band, the Royal Guard Camel Mounted Bagpipe Band was raised by Pipe Major Gavin Moffat in 1997. Later on, the RG bands were re-designated as follows:

- 1 Royal Guard Band Squadron from Royal Guard Band (South)
- 2 Royal Guard Band Squadron from Royal Guard Band (North)
- 3 Royal Guard Mounted Band Squadron from Royal Guard Mounted Band

All bands are trained to a very high standard of musical professionalism. A military choir ensemble was added to the bands. During 1984 training commenced with the Royal Guard symphony orchestra.

ROYAL MOUNTED BAND

The Diwan Palace Office had a requirement for their own band, and it was decided that it should be a mounted band (The Royal Mounted Band).

ROYAL OMAN CAVALRY

Founded in 1974 by the sultan with 20 horses, the Royal Oman Cavalry has the role of overseeing racing, show-jumping, polo and breeding programmes, and ceremonial duties are carried out for visiting dignitaries. The Firqah, which is the ceremonial squadron, was raised in 1993.

Men of the Sultan's Special Forces wearing distinctive lilac berets, gold anodized SSF cap badges, light green uniforms with lilac stable belt and black boots. (Muqaddam Ian Buttenshaw Collection)

DIWAN ROYAL STABLES

The Royal Stables are located to the west of Oman's capital Muscat and were created in 1992. Today the stables are managed and directed by Omani and international horse experts. Horse breeding takes place in the Royal Stud Farm in Salalah.

4
SULTAN'S SPECIAL FORCES (SSF)

Formed in 1977, the SSF was established, with the aid of the British SAS, as a crack independent counter-terrorism force separate from the RAO, but capable of carrying out defence tasks. At first many Dhofari, former Firqat, forces were recruited. The protracted and bitter experience of that war had convinced the Sultan that a special force was required to ensure the Sultanate had world class specialist troops to act in a counter insurgency role and for anti-terrorism. Units are located around the country and include Dhofar. SSF consists of three regiments plus some minor units. The second regiment was raised in 1986 and the third around 2012-13. SSF Headquarters are at Al Azaiba. Other locations for the SSF are near Seeb in the north and near Zeek in Dhofar. An operational base is believed to be in the Al Wusta region. One sub-unit named Cobra, specialises in Counter Terrorism (CT), and is located in both north and south Oman.

UNIFORM AND REGALIA

The SSF wear a lilac beret and stable belt. The SSF headdress badge is essentially a Dhofari leather shield with wings similar to the SAS parachute qualification badge. Camouflage kit was initially British DPM pattern but changed to a unique SSF style later.

5
THE ROYAL AIR FORCE OF OMAN (RAFO)

British requirements for air support for their military forces during the 1940s and 1950s in the Gulf States and Aden were mainly served by RAF bases at Aden, Bahrain and Sharjah in Oman. There was also a small RAF establishment on Masirah Island from 1936, as support for a forward base for flying boats. Masirah was also to have a high-frequency wireless station. RAF Salalah was constructed in 1928, and had been in use as a staging post for both military and civilian aircraft. In the 1950s Salalah was a refuelling staging post for the duty Valetta flights from RAF Khormaksar in Aden to RAF Mauripur in Pakistan, until the latter closed in 1956. Throughout the 1960s, Salalah provided refuelling and replenishment facilities for Valetta, Beverley, Argosy, Dakota and other aircraft operating on the Aden-Riyan-Salalah-Masirah-Sharjah-Bahrain routes, and could accommodate limited numbers of personnel for overnight stops.

The Jebel Akhdar campaign had shown a requirement for air support and transport but funds were short. However the Sultanate raised the Sultanate of Oman's Air Force (SOAF) in 1959 based at the Bait al Falaj airfield, Muscat. It was originally envisaged that the Sultan of Oman's Air Force (SOAF) was to support the Sultan's Land Forces in providing tactical support, troop transport, light cargo and battalion roulement between north and south. The sultanate was poor, very conservative, and oil exploration was still continuing. As of that time, the small air force was equipped with two Scottish Aviation Pioneer CC.Mk 1 light transports and three Hunting Provost T.Mk 52 trainers, which had their wings strengthened to carry 25-pdr bombs and 2-inch unguided rockets on underwing hard-points, and two Browning machine guns installed internally – all operated and maintained by British personnel. In 1960, the SOAF accepted two Provosts, another Pioneer and four De Havilland Canada DHC-3 Beaver light transports. Two Provosts and one Beaver were detached to Salalah in 1961 to support the ground forces in Dhofar. Britain provided 12 armed Percival Provost T.Mk 52s in 1962. The Provosts, Pioneers and Beavers were to carry the SOAF through the following decade.

Later in the decade Pilots could only provide limited air support from Salalah to the infantry on the Jebel. Their primary task was to deliver water, supplies and ammunition to small airstrips in the combat zone. CASEVAC flights were made when possible but fixed wing aircraft were not always able to reach casualties in difficult terrain. With the income from oil sales only just beginning to become available, the growth and modernisation was initially very slow. It was only in 1968-1970 that jet aircraft and then helicopters became available. The pace of further progress significantly increased following the coup of 1970, when Sultan Qaboos ensured that the armed forces would be expanded at a much faster rate, although being obliged to fund social developments.

As the Dhofari insurgents began deploying ever more advanced weapons of Chinese origin, in 1968 the decision was taken for the SOAF to purchase 12 British Aircraft Corporation (BAC) Strikemaster T.Mk 82s. Delivered a year later, they were again operated by British personnel seconded from the RAF or on contract. The Strikemaster's were to play a key role in the Dhofar War and their number was eventually increased to 24. Other aircraft accepted into the SOAF by the early 1970s were Douglas Dakota transports, de Havilland DHC-4 Caribous, the first out of an eventual 16 Short S.C.Mk 3 Skyvan 3Ms and five Vickers Viscount. Also of considerable use were Pilatus PC-6 Porter air ambulances, acquired and deployed later during the Dhofar War. By 1972, the SOAF had its tactical headquarters situated in Dhofar: the Strike Squadron operated Strikemasters, with six available on average (several aircraft were always undergoing periodic maintenance or repairs of combat damage); the Helicopter Squadron usually had six AB.205s and two Agusta-Bell 206s available, while the Air Support Squadron had received its first de Havilland Canada DHC-4 Caribou, and three Skyvan STOL transports. Nearly all of the SOAF personnel were still British nationals, either seconded or contracted to serve in Oman: although dozens of Omanis were being trained to become pilots, winchmen and loadmasters. Gradually their numbers increased to significant levels. Eventually, the SOAF's primary roles crystallized as those of providing strike, reconnaissance and transport support for ground forces. Nevertheless, towards the end of the conflict the service also became capable of running independent ground-strike operations against crucial targets in Yemen.

In 1974 the SOAF purchased eight Britten Norman BN.2A21 Defenders, three BAC One-Elevens, and one BAC VC.10 to be used by the Royal Flight. Squadron numbers 3 and 14 (located at Salalah and Seeb, respectively) then saw the introduction of more than 20 Augusta-Bell AB.205 helicopters. During the same period, the still relatively primitive facilities at Salalah, Masirah and Bait al Falaj were expanded for jet operations, a new air base constructed at Midway (subsequently renamed into Thumrait), and dozens of desert strips were improved. Later during the same year the commanders of the SOAF began the work on establishing an integrated air defence system (IADS) and this became operational four years later. A major

A pair of SOAF Provost T.1s during a training flight in 1960s. A total of 25 were operated by the SOAF. (Courtesy: Muqaddam Ian Buttenshaw)

RAFO headdress badge for warrant officers. (Cliff Lord Collection)

step forward in technology took place in 1976 when it was decided to introduce Rapier low level surface-to-air missiles.

On average the SOAF kept some 15-16 FGA.Mk 73A/Bs strikers, one FR.Mk 10 reconnaissance fighter, and two T.Mk 66 two-seat conversion trainers – all assigned to the newly-established No. 6 Squadron – operational, while other aircraft were used as replacements or sources of spares. By February 1975, up to 31 Hawker Hunter FGA.Mk 9s fighter and ground attack aircraft entered service: all were donated by King Hussein of Jordan. Like Iranian Phantoms, the Hunters saw their most intensive action between October and December 1975, when they ran a five-week-long strategic offensive against major supply depots and routes of the insurgency, thus indirectly supporting a joint Iranian and SAF offensive. Through repeated destruction of enemy troop concentrations, supply dumps, fortified sites and artillery positions, they not only safeguarded friendly ground forces deployed to protect

Sarfait, *Mainbrace* and *Capstan* (all of which were within range of the Yemeni artillery), but also fully exposed the vulnerability of their enemy to air attacks. Ultimately, this proved crucial for undermining the Yemeni wish to support the PFLO and the ending of the War in 1975. Although flying hundreds of attack sorties, the SOAF suffered minimal losses during the war.

With the growing efficiency of the Omani forces, the role of the SOAF became more 'strategic' and began including well planned air strikes on enemy supply lines, but also the well-protected Sherishitti Caves, one of the major insurgent bases inside the country. Meanwhile, the expansion of the SAF through the 1970s had increased the tasks for the SOAF: the two old Dakotas were replaced by new transport aircraft, including five Vickers Viscount that made troop re-deployments from north to the south of the country not only easier, but also faster. RAF Salalah was expanded to accommodate even larger passenger aircraft, and facilities constructed to enable their rapid transfer into lighter Short SC.Mk 3 Skyvan short take-off and landing (STOL) transports, capable of operating under most austere circumstances. The flexibility of the SOAF was further increased through the availability of Iranian-donated AB.205s, which enabled rapid troop movement and also CASEVAC even from the most rugged terrain: the latter factor especially proved a major morale boost for ground forces.

With cessation of hostilities, ten SEPCAT Jaguar tactical strike fighters were ordered between 1977 and 1978 enabling the surviving Strikemaster's to be used for training purposes. The first batch of Jaguars was operated by No. 8 Squadron from Thumrait AB: twelve additional Jaguars were delivered starting from 1983 to form a second unit, No. 20 Squadron, at Masirah AB. Several early warning radars and a centrally controlled communications network completed the IADS that became operational by the late 1970s. Two additional squadrons of Rapier SAMs equipped with Blindfire radars reinforced the low-level air defences by 1983. A continuing modernisation programme in the 1980s saw the IADS being further expanded and upgraded through the addition of

Martello 5713 long-range 3D radars and MACE display and data-handling systems. A new control and reporting centre was built and associated operation centres upgraded.

During the second half of the 1980s and all through the 1990s the SOAF/RAFO was further expanded on the basis of lessons from the Dhofar War, and thanks to the strengthened economy. 'Omanisation' of the air force resulted in Omani's reaching senior roles in the air force and RAF Loan Officers were reduced in numbers. Sultan Qaboos Air Academy, which opened at SOAF Masirah in 1986, provided initial officer, flying and ground training for the Royal Air Force of Oman.

The Sultan of Oman's Air Force was re-designated Royal Air Force of Oman (RAFO) in 1990. Air Vice Marshal Talib bin Miran al-Ra'isi became the first Omani to be Commander of the Royal Air Force of Oman in June 1990. There was a pressing need for the dependence on expatriate workers to gradually diminish and for them to be replaced by fully qualified Omani servicemen trained as aircraft technicians and mechanics. Air force recruits did their basic military training at the Sultan's Armed Forces Training Regiment before

Five De Havilland Canada DHC-2 Beaver AL.1 light transport aircraft were operated by the SOAF from 1961 to 1976. (Courtesy: Muqaddam Ian Buttenshaw)

SOAF Mk 82 Strikemaster Light Fighter Bomber capable of operating from rough air strips and providing close air to ground support. 1970s. (Muqaddam Ian Buttenshaw Collection)

undergoing trade training. Three C-130H Hercules were purchased to enhance the transport capability. Among their many tasks they were also used to supply an Omani battalion that served in the Saudi Arabian-led Task Force Omar as part of the GCC ground forces used to liberate Kuwait. The aircraft were based in Seeb.

Replacement of the Hawker Hunters started in 1993 and 1994 when four BAE Hawk T.Mk 103 lead-in fighter-trainers and 12 single-seat Hawk F.Mk 203 light ground attack/interceptor fighters were accepted by RAFO and were integrated into No. 6 Squadron at Masirah. The Jaguar's service life was extended into the second decade of the 21st century by major upgrades.

No. 1 Squadron provides basic training using PAC Super Mushshak primary trainers and Pilatus PC-9s. Advanced flying training is done on the Hawk. Helicopter training is provided by the Bell 206 and Super Lynx Mk 120 of No. 3 Squadron at Salalah AB. Oman ordered 20 NHI NH90 Tactical Transport Helicopters (TTH) and the first pair was delivered in 2000. January 2002 saw an order for 16 Westland Helicopters Super Lynx 300s. Delivery started in 2004 and these are operated by No. 3 Squadron at Salalah and No. 15 Squadron at al-Musana, and also by the Search and Rescue detachment at Masirah.

In May 2002, the Sultanate signed an agreement with the US government – the Peace A'sama A'safiya I programme – for the acquisition of 8 Lockheed-Martin F-16C Block 50 and 4 F-16D Block 50 multi-role jets, powered by the General Electric F110-GE-129 engines. The first aircraft to reach Oman was the F-16D serial number 801, which was accepted on 19 July 2005; the first single-seater followed in September of the same year. The F-16C/Ds are all serving with No. 18 Squadron, based at Thumrait AB. In addition to air defence and ground attack, they also had a reconnaissance role, using the Goodrich DB-110 digital real-time tactical reconnaissance system. The latter allows the crew to capture images by day or night using a digital camera enclosed in a 19ft (6m) pod carried on the centreline: photographs are fed in real time to a ground station with the help of a data-link system. A further order for another 10 F-16Cs and 2 F-16Ds was placed. Meanwhile, the first Lynx entered service in July 2004. During 2007, two Airbus A.320 Corporate Jetliners, were ordered for VIP transport duties and troop transport. These aircraft went to No. 4 Squadron. Later Omani acquisitions included EADS EF-2000 Eurofighter Typhoon jet fighters and additional British Aerospace (BAE) Hawk Advanced Jet Trainers.

Five De Havilland Canada DHC-4 Caribou transports flew with the SOAF from 1970-1977. (Courtesy: Muqaddam Ian Buttenshaw)

SOAF Agusta-Bell AB.205A-1 helicopters obtained from 1971. A total of 33 have flown with the Oman Air Force. (Muqaddam Ian Buttenshaw Collection)

engines, electrical systems, but also for operations, supply, air movement control and administration. Flying training is conducted at the Sultan Qaboos Flying Academy at Masirah, and air traffic control (ATC) training at the Aircraft Control College at Seeb. Future RAFO officers also attend the Joint Command and Staff Course at BAF and staff courses overseas. The Sultan Qaboos Air Academy (SQAA) located at RAFO Ghala is used for advanced officer training and includes a number of other squadrons: Military Training Wing, Personnel Training, Ground Defence Training, Security Police School, AFIC School, and Basic Staff Course School.

UNIFORM AND REGALIA
Sky Blue beret and light blue uniform. RAFO have their own unique style Camouflage kit.

RAFO TACTICAL OPERATIONS
Operations in Dhofar had shown that there was a requirement for an Air Force officer to be on the staff of each brigade to act as air advisor to the brigade commander and to facilitate interoperability between the Air Force and the Land Forces. The Brigade Air Support Officer and his team were responsible for all Forward Air Control, fixed-wing and rotary-wing transport and tactical support for the Land Forces in the field.

RAFO SECURITY POLICE AND FIRE SERVICE
The Royal Air Force of Oman Security Police were formed in 1975. A merger between the Security Police and the Fire Service took place in 1986 making them one branch. Tasks and role of the branch involves securing all Air Force establishments, which includes personnel, aircraft and equipment. Also provided are fire, crash and rescue facilities at the major air bases, as well as domestic fire cover and for air operations in the field. Other duties include guarding vulnerable points including installations, equipment, buildings and aircraft. Mobile, foot and dog patrols are also carried out. This unit is responsible for Air Transport Security which involves screening and processing passengers, baggage and freight travelling on RAFO aircraft.

Sub-units of RAFO Security Police and Fire Service include the Special Investigation Section which is an integral part of the Air

INFRASTRUCTURE AND TRAINING
The original RAFO Bases were located at Thumrait and Salalah, with the latter being a former RAF base, but at the time of writing housing the Sultan Qaboos Flying Academy and the Air Force Technical College. Seeb is the main transport and logistic base and the Musandam Peninsula has an air base at Khasab. No. 14 Squadron of the RAFO provides a search and rescue (SAR) detachment operating three AB.205 helicopters. Over the last 20 years two entirely new air bases have been constructed: one at al-Musana'a, 130 kilometres west of Muscat, and another at Adam, about 180 kilometres west of Muscat.

Airworks Limited (Ltd)., a civilian company, set up the original Technical Training School in Oman to train Omani recruits as mechanics in 1973. The following year the school was re-designated as the Technical Training Institute and re-located to Seeb. This institute became the Air Force Technical College (AFTC) in 1993, which has ever since provided airmen trained in the many trades required to maintain and operate a modern air force – including specialists qualified to maintain airframes, armament, aircraft

Force Security Police and was formed in 1982. Under the Director of Security and Fire, RAFO is charged with the investigation of crime and breaches of security within the entire Ministry of Defence. In addition, there is a separate Police Dog Section that has been effective since 1977, and is used to patrol airfields. A Dog Training School was established at RAFO Thumrait and Dog Sections are at all major bases.

ROYAL AIR FORCE OF OMAN BAND

The Sultan of Oman's Air Force Music was formed in 1982. Prior to this a RAF loan officer became Director of the SOAF Music in 1981. With his direction the band performed its first musical display in 1983, and also that year performed for HM Sultan Qaboos at Seeb Palace. During the following year the band participated in the National Day celebrations and in 1985 it participated in the Omani Tattoo. The band has also played at RAF Cranwell in England. In June 1990 the Sultan of Oman Air Force Music was re-designated Royal Air Force Oman (RAFO) Band. The women's section was introduced in 2008. RAFO School of Music provides training for the bandsmen where some of them play Arab instruments or sing in the Omani Music Group. Seven musicians play fanfare trumpets in the fanfare party. A full range of engagements include ceremonial parades, marching displays, public and school concerts, RAFO Dinner Nights and other internal functions. When required the band will combine with other bands for inter-service and national events. Visits to foreign countries have taken place on several occasions representing RAFO and the Sultanate. The Pipes and Drums are regular visitors to the Dubai Highland Games, where they have won a number of competitions.

During 2008 a 62 strong all-female band was formed and quickly expanded to nearly 100 musicians. The band played at the 40th National Day Oman Military Music Festival and has also played at international events including in France in 2011, Germany in 2012 and France in 2013 and again in Germany in 2014.

AIR FORCE TECHNICAL COLLEGE

Formed in 1974, the Trade Training Institute was located at RAFO Seeb. The training covered many trades including aircraft mechanics and technicians, suppliers, clerks, ground operators, assistants, and air loadmasters. Over the years the college expanded to include many more trades running technical and non-technical courses associated with on the job training. By 1993 the Trade Training Institute was re-designated as the Air Force Technical College. Additional training for aircraft engineering included airframe, engines, armoury, electrical as well as training in Operations, Air Navigation, Air Movements, Supply and Administration.

SULTAN QABOOS AIR ACADEMY

HM the Sultan opened the Air Academy at Masirah in February 1987. The academy consisted of the department of Flying Training, No. 1 Squadron, and the Department of Officer Training (which was later conducted at RAFO Ghallah).

SOAF helicopters – including Bell 206 (foreground) and AB.205, during the 1970s. (Muqaddam Ian Buttenshaw Collection)

RAFO PHYSICAL EDUCATION TRAINING SCHOOL

The Ghallah Physical Education Training School was established in 1986 along with RAFO Ghallah Sports Complex. Physical Education Instructor training courses were held as well as organized sporting events and championships. In 1990 a RAFO gymnastic team was formed and participated in a number of national and overseas events.

RAFO SQUADRONS
NO. 1 SQUADRON

Initially equipped with Strikemaster aircraft at Salalah for operational tasks, No. 1 Squadron moved to Masirah for pilot training as its Strikemasters were designed for training as well as operations. Later more modern and advanced aircraft were brought in for training purposes. Super Mushshak and PC-9(M) were introduced. The squadron is part of Sultan Qaboos Flying Academy.

NO. 2 SQUADRON

The first two Short Skyvan light transports were accepted into the air force in 1970, along with Caribous. Originally of flight-strength and based at Bait al Falaj, in 1973 the unit was eventually expanded into No. 2 Squadron. At the time of writing, the unit is currently operating the C.295MPA – a multirole maritime patrol aircraft derived from the C.295 military transport aircraft.

A Vickers Viscount airliner of the SOAF, used for VIP duties and for troop-transport in the early 1970s. (Muqaddam Ian Buttenshaw Collection)

SOAF operated three BAC 1-11 from 1971 for VIP and troop transport. (Muqaddam Ian Buttenshaw Collection)

SOAF Britten Norman BN-2A-21 Defender multi-role utility transport aircraft. Eight of which were ordered from 1974. (Muqaddam Ian Buttenshaw Collection)

but were relocated to Musana'a in 2017 when the Bell 429 helicopter was delivered.

NO. 4 SQUADRON

In 1974, the Vickers Viscount Squadron of SOAF was named No. 4 Squadron and operated out of Seeb Airport. BAC 1-11 aircraft were introduced and the Vickers Viscounts were retired at the end of 1977. A Falcon 20 of the Royal Flight joined No. 4 Squadron in August 1978. Pilot training for light tactical aircraft was also part of the role of the unit, seeking to prepare students for operations on larger and more complex aircraft like the BAC 1-11 and the C-130. At the time of writing this unit operates Airbus A.320-214CJ.

NO. 5 SQUADRON

No. 5 Squadron was formed with the arrival of the Britten-Norman Defender aircraft. Much of the squadron's role was in support of Rural Health Services where the Defender was ideal for remote locations. The squadron relocated to Salalah in 1976 and re-equipped with Short Skyvan light transports.

NO. 6 SQUADRON

Formed in 1975 at RAFO Thumrait, No.6 Squadron was equipped with Hawker Hunter fighter ground attack aircraft. The squadron was tasked with air defence for the southern part of Oman and close air support for army units. Advanced flying training was also provided for graduate pilots from the Air Academy who were selected for the Jaguar squadrons. Hawk 103s, 103As and 203s were later based with No. 6 Squadron. The squadron is now part of Sultan Qaboos Flying Academy.

NO. 8 SQUADRON

One of the roles of No. 8 Squadron when formed in June 1977 was the operational conversion of Hawker Hunter pilots onto the new Jaguar aircraft. Other tasks for the squadron were air defence for southern Oman and long-range interdiction missions and reconnaissance tasks.

NO. 3 SQUADRON

Bell 205 and 206 helicopters were introduced in 1971 at Salalah. The role of the squadron was to support the Land Forces and carry out civil aid tasks. Later, Super Lynx were operated from Salalah

One of the Hawker Hunter fighter/ground attack jets donated by King Hussein of Jordan. (Muqaddam Ian Buttenshaw Collection)

RAFO Parading their standard. The airmen are wearing the distinctive blue Air Force uniforms. Post-2000. (Courtesy: Muqaddam Ian Buttenshaw)

Close air support missions for the Army were also provided. During November 1983, the squadron was divided in strength and No. 20 Squadron was created at Masirah with new aircraft. The squadron converted to EF-2000 Typhoon aircraft in 2017-2018.

NO. 9 SQUADRON

No. 9 Squadron was established in 1977. A major reorganisation took place in 1981, when the unit received the role of providing mobile infantry support to the SOAF/RAFO Security Police as necessary, primarily for the purpose of providing defence for ground installations. The squadron also represents the air force on all ceremonial occasions and the inter service arms competitions.

NO. 10 SQUADRON

No. 10 Squadron was raised in 1977 at Thumrait. Its role was to provide air defence for SOAF Thumrait and vital installations in the southern region. The Rapier surface to air missile system was the weapon selected for the squadron.

NO. 12 SQUADRON

In 1981, No. 12 Squadron was formed at Seeb and equipped with Rapier surface to air missile systems to protect the air force base and vital installations.

NO. 14 SQUADRON

Formed on 1 March 1978, at Seeb, No. 14 Squadron was equipped with six Bell 205 helicopters. Later in 1982, Bell 206 helicopters were introduced and were used mainly in the reconnaissance role until November 1985 when they were reallocated for student pilot training at Salalah. The VIP Flight operated three Bell 212 helicopters and another one at Masirah for search and rescue. The Khasab helicopter detachment became an independent flight on 25 April 1987 although supported by No. 14 Squadron. Later the squadron was equipped with NH.90-TTH, AS.332C and SA.330J helicopters.

NO. 15 SQUADRON

The squadron has flown Westland Super Lynx Mk 120 multi-purpose twin-engine military helicopter from 2004, of which 16 were purchased.

NO. 16 SQUADRON

With the rapid development of the Sultan's Armed Forces there was a requirement to increase the capacity and capability of air transport. The first C-130 arrived at Seeb on 1 April 1981 as part of No. 2 Squadron. The C-130 flight increased and a new squadron was required for them. On 13 January 1985, No. 16 Squadron was raised. The C-130H was able to provide internal transport when first introduced including access to 26 desert air strips. The aircraft have assisted in sea searches and international disaster relief.

NO. 17 SQUADRON

The Squadron flies the NH.90-TTH helicopter which is used for tactical transport and search and rescue operations. The first pair of helicopters entered service in 2010. Twenty were on order.

NO. 18 SQUADRON

This is one of most recent units of the RAFO, equipped with 12 F-16C-50-CF and F-16D-50-CF fighter-bombers, acquired from 2005.

NO. 20 SQUADRON

Formed in November 1983, No. 20 Squadron provided post-graduate training for Omani pilots within an operational squadron environment. It was also the first unit in RAFO to train Omani ground-crew with the assistance of a team of RAF loan service technicians. The squadron was tasked with defending the airspace of northern Oman. Not only did the squadron have an air defence role but was capable of providing close air support for ground forces. Aircraft flown by the squadron included Jaguar S and B until 2014 when they were replaced with F-16C-50-CF and F-16D-50-CF. The squadron is home-based at Thumrait.

NO. 22 SQUADRON

This Squadron was formed in May 1986 at SOAF Masirah as an air defence unit using the rapier surface to air missile system.

6

ROYAL NAVY OF OMAN (RNO)

Before the Sultan of Oman's Navy there was a wing of the Oman Gendarmerie known as the Inshore Patrol Unit. Formed in 1960, the unit consisted of a single wooden dhow, *Nasr Al Bahr*, but more were to be added later. The dhows patrolled the Al Batinah coastline, ostensibly to prevent weapon smuggling and illegal immigration. Another boat was required and in 1966 the *Al Taief* was hired to carry out inshore patrols between Korea Morea Islands (Halaniat Islands) and Ras Dharbat. This dhow was replaced by *Al Muntaser*. In 1967, *Fath Alkhair* joined the service, later followed by *Al Had'r*. The first ship built was *Al Said* in 1970 and was the first Royal Yacht. *Al Said* was used for military purposes during the Dhofar war.

The Inshore Patrol Unit was the nucleus of the formation in 1971 of the Sultan of Oman's Navy (SON) and joined Sultan Armed Forces as a main service. By early 1972 the SON had a motorised dhow operating in the waters off Dhofar, which came under HQ

Al Bushra, one of three fast patrol boats, as seen in about 1975. (Muqaddam Ian Buttenshaw Collection)

Dhofar, and was tasked with troop and cargo transport, as well as interception of foreign vessels in Omani waters. Rescue at sea was also a responsibility. The role of the SON was to protect territorial waters and Sultanate shores through constant patrols to deter illegal acts and aggression, to monitor the key areas, to maintain freedom of navigation and to support the land forces. This included the Straits of Hormuz where it was to protect and direct the passage of commercial shipping, protect fisheries and maritime resources in addition to helping people requiring assistance.

In 1972, Sultan of Oman's Navy saw the launch of the Royal Ship *Dhofar*. Three fast patrol boats (*Al Bushra*, *Al Mansoor* and *Al Najah*) joined the fleet in 1973, and in the same year Sultan of Oman's Navy moved to Sultan Bin Ahmed Naval Base at Khor Al Mukalla in Muscat. In 1975, SON acquired two minesweepers (*Al Nasri* and *Al Salihi*) which had been modified to operate as regular patrol boats. After that, the fleet was supplied with 3 LCMs (Landing Craft Mechanical), *Sulhafat Al Bahr*, *Al Sansool* and *Al Doghs*. In 1978, the SON Training Centre was established in Sur. At the beginning of the 1980s, a variety of landing craft were acquired and some modifications were made to the design of *Al Said* and it was renamed *Al Mabrukah*, which was to operate as an inshore patrol ship and also as an officer training ship. In the period of 1983-1984, the fast attack missile craft *Dhofar*, *Al Sharqiyah* and *Al Batinah* were accepted into the SON. During 1986 the Ras Musandam Naval Base was opened and later renamed Musandam Naval Base. 1987 saw the SON move from Sultan Bin Ahmed Naval Base in Muscat to Said Bin Sultan Naval Base (SBSNB) in Masanah, which was officially opened on 14 November 1988. A year later the Royal Ship *Musandam* joined the fleet.

On 16 June 1990, Sultan of Oman's Navy was renamed Royal Navy of Oman (RNO). Fast gun boats *Al Bushra*, *Al Mansoor* and *Al Najah* joined the RNO in 1995 and 1996. Oman placed an order for two corvettes from Vosper Thornycroft as part of Project *Muheet* on 5 April 1992. These frigates named *Qahir Al Amwaj*, and *Al Mua'zzar* were accepted in 1996 and 1997 respectively. On 15 January 2007 the Khareef' project was signed to acquire three frigates; *Al Shamikh* which joined the RNO in 2013; *Al Rahmani* joined the service in 2014 and *Al Rasikh* was delivered in the same year. The Khareef class are three British made corvettes built by BAE Systems Maritime – Naval Ships, and operated by the Royal Navy of Oman. The ships were built in Portsmouth.

One of two ex-Dutch minesweepers operational in 1974. Launched in 1955, they were sold to Oman in 1973. *Axel M808* was renamed *Al Salini* and *Aalsmeer M811* renamed *Al Nasiri*. (Muqaddam Ian Buttenshaw Collection)

RNO letter head showing the design of the RNO metal beret badge.

RNO parading their service flag. (Muqaddam Ian Buttenshaw Collection)

Table 22: Qahir Class Corvette

Qahir Class	Corvette
Displacement	1,450 long tons (1,470 t) full load
Speed	57 km/h
Range	10,200 km
Crew	60
Armament	1 x Otobreda 76 mm 62 Super Rapid gun 2 x Oerlikon GAM-BO1 20mm cannon 1 x Octuple Crotale New Generation SAM launcher (16 missiles) 8 × MM40 Block 2 Exocet anti-ship missiles
Aircraft	None

Table 23: Khareef Class Corvette

Khareef Class	Corvette
Displacement	2,660 tonnes
Speed	52 km/h
Range	8,300 km
Complement	100
Armament	1 × 76mm Oto Melara cannon 2 × 30mm MSI DS30M 30 mm cannon 12 × MBDA VL Mica SAM 8 × MM-40 Block III Exocet SSM
Aircraft	1 helicopter – enclosed hangar

The RNO Training Centre (former SON Training Centre) was renamed Sultan Qaboos Naval Academy in 2011. Three new

RNO Band badge. (David Turner Collection)

inshore patrol vessels were ordered in 2012 and an order placed to build *Shabab Oman II*; this ship was built in Romania as a full-rigged sailing ship, and fitted out in the Netherlands. It was launched in 2014.

UNIFORM AND REGALIA
Dress distinctions: Navy blue beret. Blue and white *shemagh*. RNO have their own unique style camouflage kit.

SAID BIN SULTAN NAVAL BASE WUDAM
In the past, Muscat had been a coaling station for the merchant marine and warships. Redevelopment of the area in the 1970s resulted in the Sultan Bin Ahmed Naval Base moving to the Said Bin Sultan Naval Base in 1987 and officially opening in November 1988. It was built to enable the navy to have its own comprehensive maintenance and support facilities. The port is the home of the fleet, and the Fleet Maintenance Unit at Wudam Base is world class with considerable capacity for mechanical, electrical, electronic and weapon engineering. It includes a ship lift for ships up to 5,000 tonnes.

7

FOREIGN MILITARY ASSISTANCE DURING THE DHOFAR WAR

BRITISH MILITARY FORCES
With Sultan Qaboos becoming the new sultan from 1970, Britain pledged support to him. British military assistance included providing highly experienced officers to run the SAF, and commanding officers and junior officers for the battalions. A SAS advance party arrived along with Cracker Battery, which was a joint Royal Artillery and SAF artillery unit incorporating radar and locating equipment, to direct SAF artillery fire in the defence of RAF Salalah. RAF Regiment mortar detachments were also sent to protect RAF Salalah. To assist the fledgling SAF Engineers unit, Royal Engineers deployed to Oman to work with well drilling and

RNO Officers headdress badge (left) and rank insignia. (Cliff Lord Collection)

construction tasks for the civilian population, including schools and clinics. Later the RE were involved in combat engineer tasks. Four RAF Wessex helicopters were on loan to the Sultanate in the following year. In 1974 there were about 500 British personnel in Oman plus over 300 serving in the SAF. Some were on contract and others seconded to specialist units as well as NCO instructors. RAF Salalah, in Dhofar, was a major base used by the SOAF for both strike and supply missions which provided vital support for the SAF during the Dhofar War. The base was located on a plain by the coast but was within range of the Adoo on the Jebel. Small forts – known as Hedgehogs because of their appearance – heavily armed and made of sand-filled oil drums were placed strategically to ensure the enemy could not attack the airfield close up. With the introduction of Katyusha multiple rocket launchers by the Adoo the airfield came within range. To prevent attacks from happening Operation Diana was tasked to provide forward forts on the Jebel, thus preventing the enemy getting close enough to use their new weapons. Britain kept its forces to a minimum because of its problems in Northern Ireland, and also did not want to be perceived by some as a colonial force interfering in Arabia. However, its doctrine and expertise were critical to the success of the war. Further British assistance arrived in the form of a RAF Field Surgical Team and 23 Parachute Field Ambulance. British Army Training Teams, of SAS troops, were used for training battalions and working with Firqats.

CRACKER BATTERY (COMPOSITE ANGLO-OMANI ARTILLERY BATTERY)

Cracker Battery was a joint operation between the Royal Artillery and the Oman Artillery, which had been secretly agreed to between the Oman and British governments. The agreement was made for Britain to provide 21 all-ranks on three-month contingents to help protect Salalah airport, which was crucial for the war in Dhofar, from enemy mortar and rocket fire. Cracker contingents formed up at Larkhill in southern England where they were retrained on 25-pounder guns and procedures. Oman provided the 25-pounder guns, junior NCOs and gunners along with logistics and ammunition. Together with the British contingent they formed an integrated composite battery.

One early requirement of the Royal Artillery was Green Archer mortar locating radar; this came under Artillery Intelligence, which was known as Cracker. The radar was ideal for finding enemy mortar and RCL positions. A Sound Ranging Base was also introduced to great effect in locating Katyusha firing points.

Operating from 1 September 1971, Cracker 1's battery was located within the inner Salalah airfield perimeter. Initially the battery and command post consisted of three 25-pounder guns, which was later increased to four guns. Guarding the outer perimeter of the airport was a series of small Royal Air Force Regiment forts, called Hedgehogs, with observation officers located in them. The first five of the Cracker contingents suffered the most from in-coming fire. Cracker 6, which was deployed from December 1972 to the following March, continued to suffer RCL attacks along with the new menace of Katyusha rockets that were fired at the airport. This threat was significant as the rockets had a range of about 10 kilometres and became more and more accurate during Cracker 7's deployment and aircraft were being damaged. As an added protection the Oman Artillery provided a 5.5-inch gun to help combat the new rocket threat, and Operation Diana was launched by the SAF to install small units on the edge of Jebel to enable the Firqat to mount patrols and respond to any firing of mortars or rockets, and ultimately deny the Adoo their firing positions. The

Cracker Battery was moved forward to the outer perimeter placing them close enough to support SAF and the Forward Observation Officers on the Jebel. During Cracker 7's time, the battery became fully integrated into the SAF operations. Cracker 8 and 9 continued supporting Operation Diana and a light gun battery (75mm) was also brought in to help quell the Katyusha menace. The SAF launched several major operations in the Western Jebel. Their success significantly curtailed the insurgents' supply routes through Dhofar and neutralised many of the Adoo in the process, lessening their ability to fire on Salalah. Cracker 10, 11 and 12 remained *in situ* providing continued support to the SAF. December 1974 to April 1975 saw the final contingent, Cracker 13, deployed. The Adoo attempt to disrupt the airport was over. Apart from releasing Oman Artillery personnel to become involved with offensive operations, the Cracker Battery was able to provide excellent training for the Oman Artillery.

ABU DHABI DEFENCE FORCE

The ADDF sent two rifle squadrons to Oman to relieve the Oman Gendarmerie for service in Dhofar. In 1973, twelve Saladin Armoured Cars were sent to the SAF, and six more followed later.

DAMAVAND BATTLE GROUP & IMPERIAL IRANIAN BRIGADE GROUP IN OMAN (IIBG)

The Shah of Iran, Reza Pahlavi, sent 150 special forces operators from the Imperial Iranian Army (IIA) to Oman in November 1972, followed by four companies of special forces a month later. They were initially supported by Lockheed C-130 Hercules transports of the Imperial Iranian Air Force (IIAF), which delivered 60 loads of equipment and supplies to Salalah by the end of that year. This force became a vanguard to a brigade-sized battle group sent to aid Sultan Qaboos in the counter-insurgency war in Dhofar. As the Iranian deployment continued to grow through the addition of further units drawn from the IIA, the Damavand Battle Group came into being, supported by 32 AB.205 and AB.206 helicopters of the IIAA. In December 1973, this was charged with opening the Midway Road – a critical route linking Dhofar with the rest of the Sultanate.

By 1974, the Iranian ground contingent was officially re-designated as the Imperial Iranian Brigade Group. In October of the same year, this was replaced by SAF troops, enabling its re-deployment further west. Between December 1974 and December 1975, the Iranian brigade fought a number of small offensive operations, capturing Raykhut and then establishing the Damavand Line. While not enjoying particularly good relations with British forces deployed in Oman, and having to learn about counterinsurgency operations early on, the conventional warfare training of IIA forces served them well in the last year of the war. During Operation Hadaf, they lead the SAF brigade into a battle that ultimately crushed the insurgency. In the words of the contemporary CSAF, Major-General Ken Perkins, 'without Iranian assistance we would not have won the war'.

The Iranian contingent also made a massive contribution by the virtue of its airpower and not only helicopters, but Phantom fighter-bombers and Hercules transports greatly supplemented the SOAF, and acted as a major deterrent to Yemeni forces. Moreover, reconnaissance operations by RF-4E Phantom II reconnaissance fighters of the IIAF were providing vital intelligence. Finally, an Iranian naval task force participated in the blockade of the PFLO, thus denying the insurgents the use of the sea.

INDIAN FORCES

The Indian Army Medical Corps sent doctors and dentists to serve with the SAF throughout the war.

JORDANIAN FORCES

A battery of 25-pounders guns of the Royal Jordanian Army was sent by Jordan to Oman, and the Jordanian Forces provided junior officers with training. Jordan provided an engineer squadron from 1974 to 1977, and between March and September 1975 they laid mines on the Dhofar/Yemeni border and maintained barbed wire entanglements. The 550-strong Jordanian 91st Special Forces Battalion served in Dhofar relieving SAF during the same year and taking responsibility for the Midway Road. The Jordanians also helped the Jebel Regiment on offensive operations in the central area of Dhofar. A gift of 31 Hawker Hunter fighter-bombers were made to Oman along with a number of 25-pounder guns.

PAKISTAN FORCES

Pakistani seconded naval personnel served in the SON from 1974 until 1979. Pakistani technicians and motor transport fitters along with clerks and instrument makers were also made available to the SAF. Traditionally Baluch soldiers had been recruited from Gwadar since it was an Omani possession and after it had reverted to Pakistan.

SAUDI ARABIA

The Kingdom of Saudi Arabia supported Oman later during the Dhofar War by dispatching batteries of 105mm guns (and ammunition), 81mm mortars and teams equipped with .50 calibre machine guns.

8

ROYAL OMAN POLICE (ROP)

Small police forces existed in Muscat and Muttrah until about 1969. From around 1960 the police force consisted of approximately 20 men under an Arab officer named Lash Koran. Outside of these two towns Internal Security was the responsibility of the local *Walis* (village heads) and a force of local Askars. All Askar were responsible for basic policing, which included guarding the markets and enforcing law. Every province, or *wilaya*, in the country retained its own government-appointed *Askars*. These men were armed with old rifles and issued with ammunition belts and had no formal training or uniform. The senior rank was *Ageed Al Askar* or Colonel, and the deputy was titled *Ageed*.

During 1969, the decision was made to create a modern police force and the Oman Gendarmerie provided the first Head of Police and carried out some police functions until 1972. Although the police

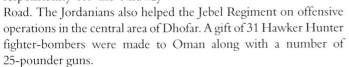

Left to right: early Muscat Police badge, Royal Oman Police cap/beret badge, and (bottom) shoulder title. (Cliff Lord)

did not originate from the OG, the 2IC of Oman Gendarmerie, Major Acutt, was appointed the first Commissioner in 1969. He was a former colonial policeman, but the recruits for the police came from SAFTC. The Police Department took responsibility of motor vehicle licensing which had previously been under the Muscat and Muttrah Municipality. Two women were recruited in 1972 to search female passengers at Beit al Falaj airport and more were recruited later in the year to work with the Directorate of Criminal Investigations. A number of women were also taken on to work for the Directorate of Prisons. However, it was not until 1974 that the first detachment of policewomen was put through the Police Training School.

Responsibility for guarding the coastline and territorial waters took effect from 1972, while the first police station at Buraimi was established a year later.

The Sultan conferred the title Royal Oman Police (ROP) on the recently formed police force in 1974 and later that year the ROP received its Colours from His Majesty the Sultan. The ROP Headquarters was opened in Qurum, Muscat, in 1975 and from 1 January the ROP took responsibility for Customs Posts. Sur Police Station opened in 1975 followed in 1976 by police stations in Masirah and Ibn.

A Police Dog Section was established on 24 September 1976. On the 9 November the first batch of Cadet Officers passed out from the Police Training School at Qurum and at the end of 1976 the Palace Police Station was opened under the Special Security Police Division. Wadi Jizzi Police Station was annexed to the Buraimi Police Division in 1977 and the Fire Training School was opened in 1979 at the Royal Oman Police Academy at Nizwa. Later known as Sultan Qaboos Academy for Police Sciences, H.M. The Sultan presented the Academy with its special Colours.

The ROP also maintains horse and camel mounted troopers who patrol terrain inaccessible to motor vehicles. The camel mounted officers operate near the Saudi-Omani border, whereas horse-mounted officers patrolled Muscat's beaches.

The Police College was established in 2000 to train ROP officers and awards diplomas and degrees in law and police sciences.

The Police Coastguard Command was equipped with a fleet of fast patrol boats including two 52-meter craft, which had a helicopter landing deck, medical assistance unit, speed boats, and could accommodate well in excess of 100 people. There was also an engineering and maintenance workshop within the Command. Sea Rescue Group was established to help prevent drowning accidents, respond to SOS calls, improve the monitoring of Oman's coastline, prevent smuggling and illegal immigration, and there was also the Oil and Gas Installations Command to protect Oman's oil and gas facilities. The Coast Guard can provide support to the Navy and the Royal Yacht fleet. A Police Coastguard training centre and a coastguard station was built at Port Sultan Qaboos.

The Police Aviation Directorate comprises several helicopters. It includes a helicopter fire-fighting service for remote areas, a flying ambulance service, and is available to provide monitoring and support services for the ROP's other departments. Ten Agusta Westland AW139 helicopters were delivered from 2005 replacing four Police Bell 214ST helicopters by 2008. Ambulance Services provide a Highway Emergency Ambulance Service for victims of road and other accidents. The police are also responsible for customs duties. The Directorate of Special Operations and VIP Protection includes The Special Task Force Command, which was raised to guard national vital points, diplomatic missions and embassies as well as VIPs. The force is also involved with bomb disposal and provides Rescue Police patrols. A free-fall parachute team takes part in security operations and also performs in free-fall parachute displays at national and police events.

Some of the other divisions in the ROP include the Mounted Police, Special Security Police, Ambulance, Juvenile Police and Financial Inquiries Division. Directorates General include Traffic, Passports and Residences, and Customs. Other Directorates General pertain only to the Royal Oman Police. These include Maintenance and Projects, Human Resources, Police Transport. ROP has its own band and an all women band.

ROP HEADDRESS

Dark blue berets are worn with some orders of dress. Police hats were first introduced in 1979. The first of these was a dark blue cap with a blue cloth flap, 32cm long and 20cm wide, to cover the neck (similar to the French 'kepi'). A white metal cap badge was placed in the front with the word 'Police' in Arabic below the state emblem. A new black hat replaced the original which was more conventional in shape. A silver coloured badge was worn on the front which had the state emblem as the central motive and the whole encompassed with leaves. Later a hatband of chequered white and dark blue squares was added to the side of the cap. Further alterations occurred with the hatband changed to black and white squares and the cap badge had a scroll with Royal Oman Police in Arabic. The present day

Muscat Police brass shoulder title. Pre 1970. (Cliff Lord Collection)

ROP hat was introduced in November 1997. Although similar to its predecessor, a new black hatband with embroidered silver geometric designs which are derived from the designs on the Omani khunjah, was accepted. The cap badge has a scroll with the words Royal Oman Police in Arabic script. ROP have their own unique style camouflage kit.

MINISTRY OF DEFENCE ENGINEERING SERVICES (MODES)

Civilians have worked for the Oman Ministry of Defence since it was formed and a small engineering group was established and named the Engineering Division, centred at Bait al Falaj Camp's Facilities and Installations Office. By 1970, due to the increase in the strength of the military forces, the Engineering Division required expanding to meet the needs of the armed forces. A large area was required for the installation of new machinery and equipment. The Engineering Division was responsible for the operation and maintenance of electrical and mechanical plants and associated equipment throughout the SAF including Air and Naval Bases. Consequently, the Division moved to Muaskar al-Murtafa (MAM) in 1976. A renaming of the Engineering Division occurred in 1987 when it became known as the Ministry of Defence Engineering Services (MODES). The establishment has grown exponentially with the growth of the armed forces. Some of the services provided now include providing electrical and mechanical engineering, public health engineering, planning, designing, tendering, contracting, and supervising all MOD projects throughout Oman. The Directorate of Logistics is responsible for purchasing, and providing equipment, transportation & plants services. MODES have their own unique style camouflage kit.

NATIONAL SURVEY AUTHORITY

Oman's National Survey Authority was created in October 1984 and is a military unit but employs many civilian cartographers. Starting as a small section, it has now grown into a large organization which prints all of Oman's map requirements. The NSA comes under the COSSAF umbrella and is based in BAF. The authority is responsible for all survey and geographic archives in Oman and also revises and provides maps, air charts and other geographic information for the Sultanate's Ministries and the Sultan's Armed and Security Forces to enable them to plan, train and protect the Sultanate's territory.

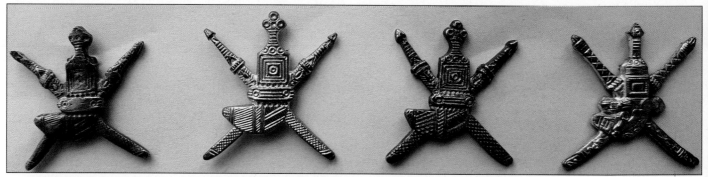

A variety of SAF headdress badges worn from about 1954 through to the 1970s and show different qualities of manufacture. Brass badges for soldiers were cast or die stamped. Officers wore silver or white metal badges. (Cliff Lord Collection)

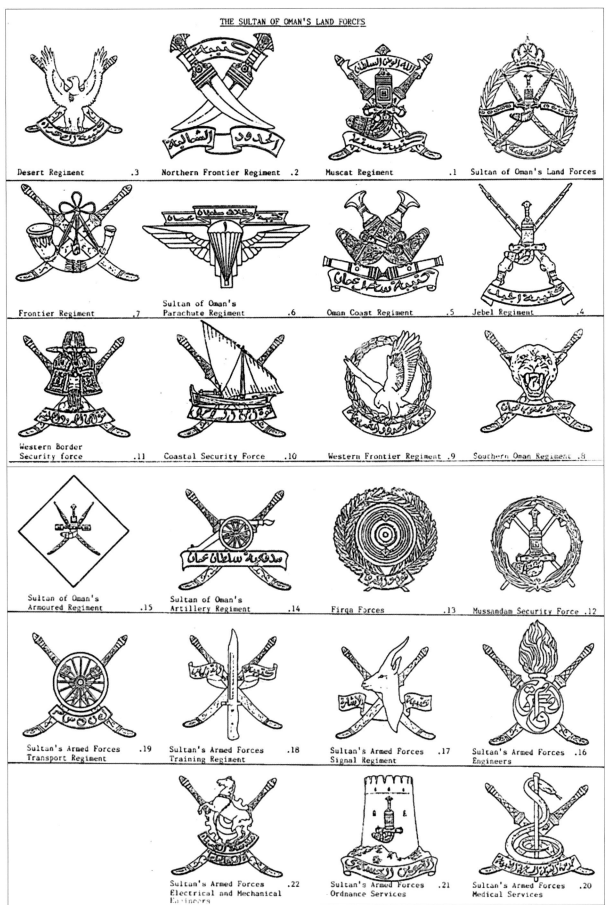

THE SULTAN OF OMAN'S LAND FORCES

Desert Regiment .3 | Northern Frontier Regiment .2 | Muscat Regiment .1 | Sultan of Oman's Land Forces

Frontier Regiment .7 | Sultan of Oman's Parachute Regiment .6 | Oman Coast Regiment .5 | Jebel Regiment .4

Western Border Security force .11 | Coastal Security Force .10 | Western Frontier Regiment .9 | Southern Oman Regiment .8

Sultan of Oman's Armoured Regiment .15 | Sultan of Oman's Artillery Regiment .14 | Firqa Forces .13 | Mussandam Security Force .12

Sultan's Armed Forces Transport Regiment .19 | Sultan's Armed Forces Training Regiment .18 | Sultan's Armed Forces Signal Regiment .17 | Sultan's Armed Forces Engineers .16

Sultan's Armed Forces Electrical and Mechanical Engineers .22 | Sultan's Armed Forces Ordnance Services .21 | Sultan's Armed Forces Medical Services .20

The regimental headdress badges were worn by the SAF from 1976-1986 although official documentation states they were introduced from 1980. The numbering of the badges reads from right to left as this is an official SAF chart. It also reflects the Order of Precedence at that time. The Frontier Regiment should read Frontier Force. Not shown in the chart is the General Service badge, which is of the same quality and size as the badges shown above. It was worn by the Oman Gendarmerie, HQ Staff, the Armoured Car Squadron, and soldiers not allocated to a regiment. The Sultan's Armed Forces Association Journal states that all of the white metal regimental badges were designed by Lt Col Andrew Kirk who was Force Director of Educational Services from 1973-1988. These badges are very well made with large lugs sweated on to the back. (Courtesy: Force Signals)

9

BADGES, DRESS REGULATIONS AND ORBAT

HEADDRESS

Force HQ officers and Artillery Troop officers wore a scarlet beret. The Artillery Troop, except officers, wore a khaki *qulla* with a red and yellow woollen *agal* until 1970 when it was replaced with the scarlet beret.

Early in 1962, CSAF, decided that all European officers throughout the army should wear a hat similar to that worn by the German Afrika Corps in WW2, known as a Forstmeister hat. An Indian tailor in Mattrah *suq* (market) was commissioned to make a quantity of these hats in khaki drill material and they were sent to all European officers. The hats were for everyday use and did not replace the scarlet Tam o' Shanter or NFR green beret for drill parades. The Muscat Regiment had a red patch behind the cap badge on the Forstmeister, and the NFR a green patch. The Forstmeister hats were poorly made and unpopular with many officers.

SHEMAGH

Red and white chequered *shemagh* were worn by the Muscat Regiment up until the start of the Dhofar War. The Oman Gendarmerie wore a blue and white chequered *shemagh*. After Sultan Qaboos's coup, the army was issued with berets for barrack wear and black on green *shemaghs* for field wear and which were tied as a simple turban. (They may have only been issued to the MR). OG continued with their blue and white shemagh.

FOOTWEAR

Various Indian Army *chaplis*, which had soles made from old motorcar tyres, were the standard footwear throughout the army in the early 1960s and were worn without socks. Black leather boots were not worn – European officers could choose to wear desert boots.

UNIFORMS AND CAMOUFLAGE KIT

Up to 1970 a sand coloured uniform was worn, which prior to deployment was hand painted to become camouflaged. In the early 1970s it was decided that the uniform should change to a dark olive green uniform that was to be worn both in the field and barracks. A stable belt was worn in barracks, and a web belt in the field. Red stable belts were worn by officers throughout the force at this time.

Some UK DPM smocks were purchased for use by guards on cold nights during the winter, but not worn in the day. These were not generally issued, but instead were held by QMs. This continued until 1985. In the Royal Review, which is a parade of the armed forces inspected by H.M. Qaboos, in October 1985 the participants were given one set of a new Oman desert style material camouflage kit which was later gradually phased in during 1985/1986. However, after the Royal Review they returned back into Olive Green's for Exercise *Raad*, but by April 1986, all of the RAO had converted to camouflage kit in their own unique Omani red/brown and black desert colours. The SOAF/RAFO had converted to their own colour of camouflage in 1978 and the RNO followed much later, in the mid-2000s. Since 1986, smocks have been issued to all ranks as personal kit in the same colours as the shirts/trousers. Every service has its own camouflage colour *shemaghs*.

Headdress badges and shoulder titles from 1990s, left to right:

Top row: SOLF headdress badge from 1986-1990; RAO headdress badge from 1990; SOAF and RAFO headdress badge.

Bottom row: Sultan's Office badge worn by civilian uniformed palace staff; current RAO headdress badge (since 1991); shoulder title (top) used by all three services in the period 1986-1990 and (bottom), since 1990.

Not shown is the RNO badge, which is similar to the latest version of the RAO badge, but includes an anchor instead of crossed rifles. Wire wove headdress badges have been worn by officers from the 1960s to the present time. (Cliff Lord Collection)

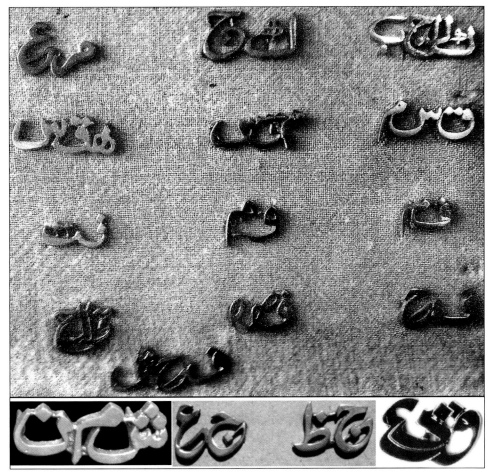

Arabic SAF Regimental Metal Shoulder titles (First Type)

(Left to right)

Top row: Oman Artillery, Jebel Regiment, Oman Coast Regiment

2nd row: Sultan's Armed Forces Engineers, Unknown, Worn by HQ SAF and all units that did not have their own shoulder title

3rd row: SAF Training Regiment, Possibly Muscat Garrison, Muscat Regt

4th row: Unknown, Desert Regt, Frontier Force

5th row: Northern Frontier Regt

6th row: Muscat Police (not part of the SAF), Oman Gendarmerie, Dhofar Gendarmerie, Armoured Car Squadron

These shoulder titles were issued from the early 1960s to existing units and to new units as they were raised. They were either brass or white metal and were replaced from 1976 onwards, officially, with the new design of Arabic titles that went with the new regimental headdress badges that started to come into use about that time. (Cliff Lord and Eddie Parks collections)

THE GENERAL SERVICE BADGE

Oman's national emblem was originally adopted from the royal emblem of the Al Said dynasty which consists of a pair of crossed swords (*Saif*) with an Omani dagger (*khunjar*) superimposed on the whole. The old Muscat Infantry had the device on their headdress badge with a scroll with 1 Muscat Infantry below. Most military badges in Oman still have the Sultanic emblem on them.

OMANI BADGES, TITLES AND PATCHES FROM THE MID-1980s

All units wore a regimental or unit shoulder patch on the left sleeve of office dress from 1986. Several of the patches have been redesigned and some new ones issued over the years. Concurrent with the introduction of the patches, regimental beret badges were replaced by a single universal SOLF headdress badge. Officers wore wire embroidered badges and other ranks metal badges. All infantry regiments changed to light grey berets (Jebel Regiment pattern). All Services (FMS, FTR, FOS, EME) had dark blue, MSO black, SOA mid blue, SAFE brown, SAF Sigs sky blue, and SOPR dark grey remaining the same. Shoulder titles remained showing the regiment's identity. Reinstatement of the original infantry coloured berets and stable belts occurred in July 1991. The universal beret badge was changed in 1990 to include a scroll with Royal Army of

---

RAO - UNIT BERET BADGES

1.   Prior to the dates below all Units wore the standard SAF/SOLF Metal Badge.

2.   Individual Unit Beret Badges were first taken into service as follows:

MR	- 5/81	MSF	- 11/84
NFR	- 2/81	FQ	- 11/81
DR	- 4/81	SOA	- 12/79
JR	- 12/80	SOAR	(SAF/ SOLF Badge since forming in 1971)
OCR	- 6/81	SAFE	- 2/81
SOPR	- 11/84	SR	- 2/81
FF	- 4/81	SAFTR-	2/81
KJ	- 2/81	FTR	- 11/80
WFR	- 11/81	FMS	- 2/81
WBSF	- 11/84	FOS	- 11/80
CSF	- 11/84	EME	- 2/81

(All Ranks wore metal badges until mid 1984 when cloth badges for officers were introduced)

3.   All Units went to standard SOLF Badge in July 1986, when individual Unit Beret Badges were done away with. Officers had embroidered cloth badges, other ranks had anodised badges. Shoulder Badges were introduced to show unit identity.

RAO Unit Beret Badges official dates of introduction of individual badges. (Cliff Lord Collection)

Table 24: Royal Army of Oman Beret, Lanyards, Badge Backings, & Stable Belt Colours

		RAO UNIFORMS		
UNIT	BERET	LANYARD	STABLE BELT	BADGE BACKING
HQ RAO	Red	Thin single strand red/green colour	Red	Nil
Bdr Gd Bde	Bright yellow	Bright yellow	Half bright yellow (top), half sand colour (bottom)	Red/green/blue backings for 1/2/3 Bns respectively
MSO	Black	Black woven, two strand	Dark green with thick black central stripe	Nil
SOA	Mid blue	White woven	Half red (top), half navy blue	Nil
Firqat Forces	Light green	Single strand light/dark green woven	Dark green with light green central stripe (equal size)	Nil
SAF Sigs	Sky blue	Sky blue woven	Sky blue	Nil
SAFE	Choc brown	Chocolate brown wove double strand	Chocolate brown	Nil
SAF Tpt	Navy blue	Woven navy blue and red, several strands	Navy blue with two thin red stripes	Nil
FOS	Navy blue	Woven navy blue/red single strand	Red with blue central stripe (equal size)	Nil
EME	Navy blue	Woven single strand, blue, yellow, red	Blue with red equal size central, thin yellow on each side of red	Nil
FMS	Navy blue	Thick woven maroon with single strand	Maroon with two thin stripes light blue (top) and navy blue	Nil
SOP	Dark grey	Maroon double strand	Dark grey with thick maroon central stripe	Nil
MR	Red (Tam O'Shanter type)	Red woven double strand	Red	Red ribbon rosette
NFR	Rifle green	Rifle green woven double strand	Rifle green	Nil
DR	Sand yellow	Sand yellow single strand	Sand yellow	Nil
JR	Grey	Woven grey double strand	Grey	Nil
OCR	Black	Blue and black woven single strand	Blue with equal size black central stripe	Blue felt square
FF	Khaki	Woven khaki double strand	Khaki	Nil
KJ	Dark green	Dark green and burnt orange double strand woven	Dark green with two thin burnt orange stripes in centre	Burnt orange felt square
WFR	Lime green	Lime green double strand	Lime green	Nil
WBSF	Green khaki	Green khaki double strand	Green khaki	Green khaki ribbon rosette
CSF	Green khaki	Green khaki double strand	Green khaki	Green khaki ribbon rosette
MSF	Green khaki	Green khaki double strand	Green khaki	Green khaki ribbon rosette
Gar MAM	Red	Thick green/red woven two strand	Red (HQ RAO)	Nil

HQ SOLF, HQ SOM Bde, HQ NOM Bde, SAFTR, KSQA, JBTC, Mounted SOLF Band and PENSEC reverted back to red berets in July 1991 when infantry battalions went back to their original colours.

Oman. At the same time a new RAO universal shoulder title was introduced. The beret badge was redesigned in 1992 and the HQ RAO shoulder title issued.

RIFLES

Firearms used post-WW2 changed from the .303 Lee Enfield, which was used until the early 1970s, and then to the British 7.62mm SLR, however the FN rifle was used in Dhofar in 1969. By the late 1970s, nearly all units had the FN, which remained in service until 1982 when the Austrian Steyr was introduced, and is still in use in the RAO. The SSF and RGO use the M16. The RAO keep 5,000 M16 rifles for drill purposes only because the Steyr is not considered to be of sufficiently smart appearance on large parades.

SAF BADGE BACKINGS PRE JULY 1986

Prior to 1986, when Unit Badges were discontinued, several units had had cloth underlays or backings to their badges, a number of which were discontinued in 1986. The following is a list of some of those backings:

- MR: Red ribbon rosette backing
- NFR: Officers wore a red backing
- JR: Black Diamond shape backing
- SOPR: Maroon backing
- ORF/ORR: Lime Green Triangular Backing
- KJ: Burnt Orange (Same as Dhofar Gendarmerie)
- WBSF/CSF/MSF: Green Khaki Ribbon Rosette
- Firqat Forces: Dark Green triangle
- SOAR: Black Diamond shape
- FSigs: Light Blue Square
- SOA: Black Square
- FTR: Red Square
- SAFTR: Bottle Green Square
- FMS: Maroon Square

TACTICAL SIGNS (TAC SIGNS) OF OMANI MILITARY VEHICLES

Official tactical signs were used circa 1978. Service and MOD vehicles displayed TAC Signs on the front nearside and the rear offside of vehicles. They were seven inches square unless otherwise stated.

ROYAL GUARD REGIMENT:

- All vehicles: Maroon background 13 and a half by 7 inches. White vehicle number in Arabic on either side of concentric circles; inner circle red: 3¼-inch diameter, Outer circle green: 5 inches diameter. White national crest and RGR monograph superimposed centrally with gold crown on top of the crest.

SULTAN OF OMAN ARMED FORCES

- HQ Sultan of Oman's Land Forces: Red/light blue/dark blue in three equal horizontal stripes in order given reading from the top.
- HQ Southern Oman Brigade: Black with white St Andrew's Cross superimposed.
- HQ Northern Oman Brigade: Red with white St Andrews' Cross superimposed.
- Muscat Regiment: Red.
- Northern Frontier Regiment: Dark green.
- Desert Regiment: Dark sand with black border.
- Jebel Regiment: Grey.
- Oman Coast Regiment: Black.

Oman RAO Lt Col rank insignia and current shoulder title on fawn epaulet. (Courtesy: Cliff Lord)

Mowag Piranha II – the so called 'Desert Piranha', in its turret variant. (Muqaddam Ian Buttenshaw Collection)

- Oman Artillery Regiment: Red/dark blue horizontally halved, red uppermost.
- Frontier Force: White/black horizontally halved, from top left to bottom right, white uppermost.
- Southern Oman Regiment: Red/green diagonally halved from top left to bottom right, red uppermost.
- SAF Training Regiment: Light green with red bayonet six inches high, centrally placed.
- Signal Regiment: White/dark blue horizontally halved, white uppermost.
- Armoured Force of Oman: Dark green with six-inch by six-inch Sultanic emblem in black centrally placed.
- SAF Engineers: Dark brown with white bursting bomb over white crossed swords (total area motif is six inches by six inches) centrally placed.
- Garrison Muaskar al Murtafa: Light green/red/light green in three equal horizontal stripes.
- Western Frontier Regiment: Orange/green quartered in order from left to right: top to bottom; orange/green; green/orange.
- Southern Oman Brigade Training Centre: Light blue/grey/green equal horizontal stripes in order given from top, with central stripe having two equally spaced triangles, combined width six-inches, with apex protruding halfway into blue, representing two hill peaks.

Annex A to
LF/PS 1141/P100
Dated 5 Jul 86

BERETS BELTS LANYARDS

Unit	Now Beret	Belt	Lanyard	Future Beret	Belt	Lanyard	Remarks
HQ SOLF HQ SOM Bde HQ NCM Bde SAFTR, KSOA JAETC, MTD SOLF Band	.... Red			.....Light Grey			
Infantry incl HQ FQ, ORF, PENSEC	.. Various			.... Light Grey			
SOPR	... mid grey/marocn..			......no change			
SOAR	... green/black			black	green/ black	green/ black	new lanyard
SOA	red	red/mid blue	white	mid blue	red/mid blue	white	beret to match blue of belt
SAFE	......brown........			......no change.......			
SR	...royal blue			..... no change			lanyard on right shoulder
FMS	red	maroon	maroon	dark blue	maroon	maroon	) Sp Services) in same) beret.) Same) colour as) FTR now) but less) red badge) flash.))).)))
FTR	dark blue	dark blue/ red	dark blue/ red	dark blue	no change		
FOS	red	red/ blue	red/ dark blue	dark blue	no change		
EME	red	dark blue/ red/ yellow	as belt	dark blue	no change		
ACS	red	red	red/ green	dark blue	....light grey ...		
Offices of CDS and HE The US Gar MAM Gar Salalah SAF IMU	red	red	red/ green	..... no change			

The official regulation on Beret Belts and Lanyards from 1986. (SOLF Dress Regulations. Annex A to LF/PS 1141/P100 dated 5 July 86)

Table 25: Royal Army of Oman Rank Structure		
Abbreviation	Fareeq Awal	General
	Fareeq	Lieutenant-General
	Liwa	Major-General
	Ameed previously Zayeem	Brigadier
	Aqeed	Colonel
Mqm	Muqaddam	Lieutenant-Colonel
	Raaid	Major
Nqb	Naqeeb previously Raees	Captain

Table 25: Royal Army of Oman Rank Structure		
Mul/1	Mulazim Awal	Lieutenant
Mul/2	Mulazim Thani	2nd Lieutenant
Wkl/1	Wakeel Awal	Warrant Officer 1 (RSM)
Wkl/2	Wakeel Thani	Warrant Officer 2
Rqb/1	Raqeeb Awal	Staff Sergeant
Rqb	Raqeeb	Sergeant
Arf	Areef	Corporal
Nb Arf	Naib Areef	Lance-Corporal
(Rukn after a senior officer's rank indicates Staff College Training)		

A trio of Hunting Provost T.Mk 52s diverted from British Army Air Corps' stocks, and a group of seconded RAF personnel formed the original inventory of the Sultanate of Oman Air Force. (Claudio Toselli Collection)

A quartet of DHC-2 Beavers diverted from British Army Air Corps stocks represented the first major reinforcement for the SOAF: with road communications virtually non-existent, their services in the form of troop transportation and the logistic support of Army outposts, and their ability to operate from most primitive airstrips made of sand, gravel, crushed rock, and dust, were of crucial importance. (Henrik von Brokhuisen Collection)

Arabic SAF Shoulder Titles (Second Type) introduced from 1981

top to bottom and left to right:

Muscat Regiment, Northern Frontier Regt, Desert Regt

Jebel Regt, Oman Coast Regt, Sultan of Oman's Parachute Regt, Frontier Force

Southern Regt, Western Frontier Regt, Coastal Security Force, Western Border Security Force

Firqah Forces, Sultan of Oman's Artillery, Sultan of Oman's Armoured Regiment, Sultan's Armed Forces Engineers

Sultan's Armed Forces Signal Regt, Sultan's Armed Forces Training Regt, Sultan's Armed Forces Transport Regt, Sultan's Armed Forces Medical Services

Sultan's Armed Forces Ordnance Services, Sultan's Armed Forces Electrical & Mechanical Engineers, Sultan's Armed Forces General Service

Sultan's Special Force, Sultan of Oman's Air Force, Royal Air Force of Oman

Royal Guard 1st type

Royal Guard 2nd type

(Cliff Lord Collection)

Table 26: Overview of diverse military units since 1921 of the Sultanate of Muscat and Oman and the Sultanate of Oman

Unit	From	To	Remarks
Muscat Levy Corps	1921	1931	To Muscat Infantry
Muscat Infantry	1931	1957	To Muscat Regiment
Artillery Section	1931	1942	To Artillery Troop
Artillery Troop	1942	1960	To Artillery Battery
Batinah Force	1953	1957	To Northern Frontier Regiment
Muscat and Oman Field Force (MOFF)	1953-1954	1957	To Oman Regiment (disbanded July 1957)
Muscat Armed Forces	1955	1958	Renamed Sultan's Armed Forces
Training Depot	1955	1962	To SAF Training Centre
Dhofar Force (Joins SAF 1970)	1955	1970	To Dhofar Gendarmerie
Signalling Detachment	1955	1961	To Signal Troop
EME Workshop	1957		Bayt al Falaj closed in 1973 and moved to MAM
Muscat Regiment	1957		From Muscat Infantry
Northern Frontier Regiment	1957		From Batinah Force
Oman Regiment	1957	1957	From Muscat & Oman Field Force survivors to Northern Frontier Regiment
Sultan's Armed Forces Army 1958 to 1977 Air Force 1959 to 1990 Navy 1971 to 1990	1958	1977	The land component of the SAF re-designated Sultan of Oman's Land Force (SOLF) in 1977, SOLF re-designated Royal Army of Oman in 1990. The Sultan of Oman's Air Force (SOAF) re-designated Royal Air Force of Oman (RAFO) in 1990. Sultan of Oman's Navy (SON) re-designated Royal Navy of Oman (RNO) in 1990.
Jebel Akhdhar Battle Training Camp (JABTC)	1959		Company Base until 1975 then Training Camp established
HQ Motor Transport Platoon	1959	1975	To AFM Transport
Oman Gendarmerie	1959	1978	To Oman Coast Regiment. OG consisted of 3 Sectors in the 1960s for garrison and reserve duties. In 1969 provided 1st Head of Police and carried out some Police functions until 1972. The OG Palace Sector (PALSEC) raised in 1970 but renamed F Sqn OG in 1972. Became the Royal Guard Sqn in 1973. D Squadron provided personnel for the new Parachute Squadron in 1975. A new Sqn raised for Peninsular Sector (PENSEC) in Musandam 1971. Southern Sector (SOUSEC) raised 1971. Western Sector (WESSEC) circa 1963. 1960 Coastal Patrol part of OG.
Sultan of Oman's Air Force (SOAF)	1959	1990	Became Royal Air Force of Oman RAFO
Oman Intelligence Service	1959	1974	To Oman Research Department
Coastal Patrol	1960	1970	Part of OG. To Sultan of Oman's Navy
Artillery Battery	1960	1971	To Artillery Regiment
Oil Installation Police	1960s	1974	Trained and administered by OG but paid for by PDO. Renamed Oil Installation Guard in early 1970s and transferred to Royal Oman Police in 1974.
Independent Guard Unit	1961	1961	Established after MR moved to Bid Bid. Prior to 1961 the MR provided Guards for Muscat. The unit was re-designated Muscat Garrison Guard Coy (MUSGAR).
Muscat Garrison Guard Coy (MUSGAR)	1961	1970s	To MAM Guard Company and BAF Garrison Guard
Ordnance Section	1961	1964	To Ordnance Depot
Signal Troop	1961	1972	To Signal Squadron North
Force EME officer appointed	1962		First officer appointed
SAF Training Centre (SAFTC)	1962	1971	From Training Depot. To SAF Training Regiment
Ordnance Depot	1964	1969	To Force Ordnance Depot (FOD)
Motor Transport Platoon	1965	1975	To AFM Transport, later FTR 1980

Table 26: Overview of diverse military units since 1921 of the Sultanate of Muscat and Oman and the Sultanate of Oman

Unit	From	To	Remarks
Desert Regiment	1966		From Red Coy Northern Frontier Regiment
Baluch Training Company	1966	1966	To B Coy Desert Regiment
Salalah Signal Troop	1967	1972	From original Signal Troop, Detachment Salalah. To Salalah Signal Squadron aka Signal Squadron South
Medical Training Centre	1967	1969	To Force Medical Unit
Sultan's Armed Forces Medical Unit (FMU)	1969	1973	To Force Medical Services
Force Ordnance Depot (FOD)	1969	1973	From Ordnance Depot. To BOD.
Ordnance Maintenance Park Thumrait	1969	1971	Renamed (1 OMP) in 1971
Muscat Guard Unit, Dhofar Wing. (MUSGAR) later known as Z Independent Coy	1969	1975	Permanently at Salalah for airfield protection. Baluch unit from Muscat Guard Unit. Under Major Spike Powell.
Baluch Askaris	1969	1971	To guard Salalah Perimeter. Later Baluch Guard and became FF in 1973.
Jebel Regiment	1970		
Artillery Training Troop	1970		Located at Suwaiq
Dhofar Gendarmerie	1970	1974	From Dhofar Force. To Kateeba Janoob (Southern Regiment)
SAF Motor & Animal Transport	1970	1975	To SAF Transport Regiment. Donkey Platoons were always independent and not attached to FTR.
1 Ordnance Maintenance Park	1971	1975	From Ordnance Maintenance Park. To Combat Supplies Pl (C Sups P).
Sultan of Oman's Navy (SON)	1971	1990	From Coastal Patrol of OG. To Royal Navy of Oman.
Sadh Defence Force	1971	1971	Became Gamel Abdul Nasser Firqat in 1971. Approx. 60 strong.
SAF Mechanical Workshops		1974	To SAF Electrical Mechanical Engineers
Dhofar Area HQ	1971	1972	To Dhofar Brigade, later SOM Bde 1976, 11 Inf Bde 1991
Baluch Guard (700 strong)	1971	1973	From Baluch Askari's in Dhofar. To Frontier Force
Firqat 28 Firqat in total	1971		Firqat Salahdin (First Firqat raised) Firqat Bayt Said Firqat Al Nassir Firqat Al Asifa Firqat Khalid bin Walid Firqat Gamel Abdul Nasser (ex SDF) Firqat Mutaharika Firqat Qaboos (previously Jaboob) Firqat Socotri Firqat Tariq bin Ziyad Firqat Ummr al Kitab Firqat Umri Firqat Western Mahri
Armoured Car Squadron	1971	1978	From Dhofar Gendarmerie. Renamed Armoured Force of Oman in 1978 to Sultan of Oman Armoured Regiment 1981.
SAF Training Regiment	1971		From SAF Training Centre (SAFTC)
Oman Artillery (OA)	1971	1980	From Artillery Battery. To Sultan of Oman's Artillery.
Potential Officer Training Wing (POTW) within the SAFTR	1971	1981	To Potential Officers Training Unit or Wahidat Tadreeb al Muashaheen (WTM). Later KSQA 1986.

Table 26: Overview of diverse military units since 1921 of the Sultanate of Muscat and Oman and the Sultanate of Oman

Unit	From	To	Remarks
2 Ordnance Maintenance Park (2 OMP)	1971	1976	Salalah. To Forward Ordnance Depot (FOD)
Dhofar Motor Transport Platoon	1971	1974	To AFMT Regiment
Electrical and Mechanical Engineers	1972		From Force Mechanical Workshops
Dhofar Brigade	1972	1976	From Dhofar Area HQ. To Southern Oman Brigade.
Northern Signal Squadron	1972	1973	From Northern Signal Troop. To Signal Regiment.
Southern Signal Squadron	1972	1973	From Salalah Signal Troop. To Signal Regiment.
Airworks Technical Training School	1973	1974	To Air Force Technical Training Institute
Frontier Force	1973		From Baluch Guard
Force Medical Services (FMS)	1973		From Force Medical Unit
SFE Engineer Troop	1973-1974	1975	Gradually expanded to Squadron size. Renamed SAFE and expanded to Regiment in 1982.
Base Ordnance Depot (BOD)	1973		From Base Ordnance Depot and Ordnance Maintenance Park
Royal Guard Squadron (later Regiment)	1973	1975	From F Sqn OG. Now separate from Sultan's Armed Force. Later Royal Guard of Oman.
HQ Northern Oman Command	1973	1976	To Northern Oman Brigade
Base Ordnance Depot MAM	1973		
Signal Regiment	1973		Including Northern Signal Squadron, Southern Signal Squadron, HQ Squadron. Support Signal Sqn formed from a division of Northern Signal Sqn.
Force HQ Force Ordnance Depot moved from BAF to MAM	1973		FOD became BOD, HQ FOS moved in 1978
Air Force Technical Training institute	1974	1993	From Airworks Technical Training School. To Sultan Qaboos Air Academy (SQAA).
Sultan's Force Engineers (SFE) 1 Field Troop SFE	1974	1976	Combat Engineers 1 Fd Troop SFE. To SFE Engineer Squadron.
Askar Force (later renamed Northern Oman Border Scouts)	1974	1976	Under Command of OG. To Royal Oman Police.
Dhofar Brigade	1974	1976	From Dhofar Area HQ. To Southern Oman Bde.
School of Signals	1974		Part of Signal Regiment's Support Sqn with Base Radio Workshop and QM
Southern Oman Regiment	1974		From Dhofar Gendarmerie. The Regiment is known as KJ, short for Kateeba Janoob Oman.
Oman Research Department	1974	1987	To Internal Security Services
Sultan of Oman's Armed Forces School	1974		
D Parachute Squadron Oman Gendarmerie. Re-designated D (Para) Sqn when trained.	1975	1978	To Oman Coastal Regiment in 1978 and then Oman Parachute Sqn (OPS) in same year. OPR in 1982, SOPR in 1985 and SOP 1993.
2 SFE Fd Troop	1975	1976	To Sultan's Force Engineer Squadron
Royal Guard Regiment	1975	1981	From Royal Guard Squadron. To Royal Guard Brigade Later Royal Guard of Oman.
Armed Forces Motor Transport (AFMT)	1975	1980	From 3 transport platoons To FTR.
Dhofar Guard Unit	1975	1976	To WFR
Artillery North	Circa 1976	1980	All artillery in Oman controlled from HQ SOA in the north
Artillery South	Circa 1976	1980	One light regiment remained based in the south following the Dhofar War on a 2 year tour

Table 26: Overview of diverse military units since 1921 of the Sultanate of Muscat and Oman and the Sultanate of Oman

Unit	From	To	Remarks
Western Frontier Regiment	1976		From Dhofar Guard Unit and Z Company
SFE Engineer Squadron	1976	1977	To Sultan's Armed Forces Engineers
HQ Northern Oman Brigade	1976	1991	From HQ Northern Oman Command. To 23 Infantry Brigade
Southern Oman Brigade	1976	1991	From Dhofar Brigade. To 11 Infantry Brigade.
Combat Supplies Platoon	1976	1976	Disbanded
Force Ordnance Depot Salalah	1976	1997	From 2 OMP. To Ordnance Depot UAG.
SOLF	1977	1990	3 Services Independent
SOLF Band	1977	1990	To RAO Band
Sultan's Special Force	1977		Independent unit. Later Bde Gp size.
Sultan's Armed Forces Engineers (SAFE)	1977	1982	Sultan's Armed Forces Engineer Regiment
Sultan of Oman's Land Force	1977	1990	From SAF. Later Royal Army of Oman.
Command Training Centre	1978	1983	Renamed Madrasat Tadreeb A'Dhubart (MTD)
EME School	1978		Evolved from a small Training Wing in the Workshops in 1957
SON Training Centre	1978	2011	Renamed RNO Training Centre in 1990. To Sultan Qaboos Naval Academy.
SAFTR MT Platoon		1978	To AFT
Armoured Force of Oman	1978	1981	From Armoured Car Squadron
Oman Coast Regiment	1978		From Oman Gendarmerie
Oman Parachute Squadron (OPS)	1978	1982	Re-designated Oman Parachute Regiment (OPR)
Operations Company	1979	1989	To Oman Reconnaissance Force (ORF) in 1983, and Oman Reconnaissance Regiment in 1989.
1 Field Regiment Oman Artillery	1980	1980	To 1 Sultan of Oman's Artillery
Sultan of Oman's Artillery	1980		From Oman Artillery
1 Sultan of Oman's Artillery (1SOA)	1980		From 1 Field Regiment OA. Light Regiment.
2 Sultan of Oman's Artillery (2SOA)	1980		From 1 Field Regiment OA. Light Regiment.
HQ Transport Squadron	1980		Formed in MAM
Sultan's Armed Forces Transport Regiment (FTR)	1980	1984	From AFM Transport. FTR split into two regiments.
Musandam Security Force	1980		Company sized. Became a battalion sized unit in 2004.
Mobile Firqat Force	1980	1983	Included Operations Company and a new company. To Oman Recce Force in 1983, to ORR in 1989.
Oman Tank Force (OTF)	1980	1981	To Sultan of Oman's Armoured Regiment
Western Border Security Force	1980		Company sized reconnaissance unit at Al Qabil
Coastal Security Force	1981		Company sized reconnaissance unit at Sur
Firqat Regularised	1981		1 part became a regular SAF regiment and the other a rural militia
Sultan of Oman's Armoured Regiment (SOAR)	1981	1991	From Armoured Force of Oman & Oman Tank Force. Later Sultan of Oman's Armour (MSO).
HQ PENSEC	1981	Late 1980s	To HQ Musandam Sector
Royal Guard Brigade	1981	1987	From Royal Guard Regiment. To Royal Guard of Oman.
Wahidat Tadreeb al Muashaheen (WTM)	1981	1986	From POTW Wing SAFTR. To Sultan Qaboos Military Academy or Koliyat Sultan Qaboos al Askariya (KSQA).
SAF Engineer Regiment	1982		From SAFE
Oman Parachute Regiment (OPR)	1982	1985	To Sultan of Oman's Parachute Regiment
SOAF Band	1982	1990	To RAFO Band

Table 26: Overview of diverse military units since 1921 of the Sultanate of Muscat and Oman and the Sultanate of Oman

Unit	From	To	Remarks
Oman Reconnaissance Force (ORF)	1983	1989	From Mobile Firqat Force. To Oman Reconnaissance Regiment.
SON Band	1983	1990	To RNO Band
Madrasat Tadreeb A'Dhubart (MTD)	1983		Officers Training School. From Command Training Centre.
1 Transport Regiment	1984		From FTR
2 Transport Regiment	1984		From FTR
EME Force Mobile Workshop	1984		
2 Signal Regiment	1985		
Force telecommunications Equipment Workshop	1985		
Force Communications Equipment Depot	1985		
Sultan of Oman's Parachute Regiment (SOPR)	1985	1993	From Oman Parachute Regiment (OPR). To Sultan of Oman's Parachute (SO Para).
Armed Forces Hospital (Al Khoudh)	1985		
Force HQ Signals	1986		
Ordnance Stores Company	1986		
Sultan Qaboos Military Academy or Koliyat Sultan Qaboos al Askariya (KSQA)	1986		From WTM
Madrassat Tadreeb Al Murashaheen (MTD)	1986		School of officer cadets
Madrassat Tadreeb Aslihat Al Isnad al Wa A'Tab (MTS)	1986		School of Support Weapons Training
Physical Education School	1986		
Sultan's Armed Forces Transport	1986		Rename of FTR
Command & Staff College	1986		Under COSSAF
Royal Guard of Oman	1987		From Royal Guard Brigade
RAFO Air Academy	1987		
3 Sultan of Oman's Artillery (3SOA)	1988		Medium Regiment
Oman Reconnaissance Regiment	1989		From Oman Reconnaissance Force
Royal Army of Oman (RAO)	1990		From Sultan of Oman's Land Force (SOLF)
Royal Air Force of Oman (RAFO)	1990		From Sultan of Oman's Air Force (SOAF)
Royal Navy of Oman (RNO)	1990		From Sultan of Oman's Navy (SON)
Mudarraat Sultan Oman (MSO) Sultan of Oman's Armour	1991		Name change from Sultan of Oman's Armoured Regiment
23 Infantry Brigade	1991		From Northern Oman Brigade
11 Infantry Brigade	1991		From Southern Oman Brigade
School of Transport	1991		
4 Sultan of Oman's Artillery (4SOA)	1992		AD Regiment
Sultan of Oman's Parachute (SO Para)	1993		From SOPR
Air Force Technical College	1993		From Air Force Technical Training Institute
2 SSF Regiment	1996		

Table 26: Overview of diverse military units since 1921 of the Sultanate of Muscat and Oman and the Sultanate of Oman

Unit	From	To	Remarks
Ordnance Depot UAG	1997		From FOD Salalah
School of Ordnance and Administration	2002		From Ordnance Training School and Administration School
Bio-Medical Workshop	2003		(EME) A small section had existed in Hospital from 1984
3 Signal Regiment	2003		
1 Border Guard Regiment	2008		Within Border Guard Brigade
2 SAFE Regiment	2008		From the original SAFE Regiment dividing in two
Border Guard Brigade	2009		
2 Border Guard Regiment	2009		Within Border Guard Brigade
3 Border Guard Regiment	2011		Within Border Guard Brigade.
Sultan Qaboos Naval Academy	2011		From SON/RON Training Centre
3 SSF Regiment	Circa 2012		

The workhorse of the SOAF in the 1970s were Agusta-Bell 205s of the Helicopter Squadron and Skyvan 3Ms: the two types fulfilled a variety of roles, ranging from troop-transport, assault and CASEVAC to reconnaissance. A single Skyvan could load anything from goats, sheep or donkeys to 1,815kg (4,000lbs) of ammunition or medical supplies, or a Land Rover. (Albert Grandolini Collection)

A classic photograph of one of the first nine Strikemaster T.Mk 82s acquired by the SOAF in the early 1970s (serial 404/4). Notable are underwing 'banks' of Sura unguided rockets, and 250lb bombs. Firepower of SOAF Strikemasters was often of crucial importance for the outcome of dozens of clashes with the 'Adoo' – and thus the entire war in Dhofar. (Claudio Toselli Collection)

BIBLIOGRAPHY

A Short History of the Royal Air Force Regiment, (Ramsgate: R.A.F. Regiment Fund, 1974).

Allfree, P.S., Warlords of Oman, (London: Robert Hale, 1967).

Barr, James, Lords of the Desert: Britain's Struggle with America to Dominate the Middle East, (London: Simon & Schuster, 2018).

Beasant, John, Oman: The True-Life Drama and Intrigue of an Arab State, (Edinburgh: Mainstream Publishing Company, 2002).

Buttenshaw, Ian, The Royal Army of Oman and its Units: A Brief History, (Oman: RAO Publications, 2010). Cole, Roger, & Belfield, Richard, SAS Operation Storm: The SAS Under Siege, Nine Men Against Four Hundred, (London: Hodder & Stoughton Ltd., 2011).

Gardiner, Ian, In the Service of the Sultan: A First Hand Account of the Dhofar Insurgency, (Barnsley: Pen and Sword Military, 2010).

Hoskins, Alan. A Contract Officer in the Oman, (Tunbridge Wells: DJ Costello Publishers Ltd, 1998).

Lee, Air Chief Marshal Sir David, GBE CB, Flight from the Middle East: A History of the Royal Air Force in the Arabian Peninsula and adjacent Territories 1945-1972, (London: HMSO, 1980).

Lord, Cliff and Birtles, David, The Armed Forces of Aden and the Protectorate 1839-1967, (Solihull: Helion & Company, 2011).

Lord, Cliff and Watson, Graham, The Royal Corps of Signals: Unit Histories of the Corps 1920-2001 and its Antecedents, (Solihull, Helion and Company, 2003).

Lunt, J.D., Imperial Sunset: Frontier Soldiering in the 20th Century, (London: Macdonald Futura, 1981).

Oliver, K.M., Through Adversity: The History of the Royal Air Force Regiment, 1942-1992 (Rushden: Forces & Corporate, 1997).

Peterson, J.E, Defending Arabia, (London: Croom Helm, 1986).

Peterson, J.E., Oman's Insurgencies: The Sultanate's Struggle for Supremacy, (London: SAQI, 2007).

Pivka, Otto von, Armies of the Middle East, (London: Book Club Associates, 1979).

Priestland, J., (ed.), The Buraimi Dispute: Contemporary Documents 1950-1961, Volume 5: 1954-1955 (Farnham Common: Archive Editions Limited, 1992).

Ray, Bryan, Dangerous Frontiers: Campaigning in Somaliland & Oman, (Barnsley: Pen & Sword Books, 2008).

Thwaites, Peter, Muscat Command, (London: Leo Cooper, 1995).

Winner, Pete, & Kennedy, Michael Paul, Soldier 'I': The Story of an SAS Hero, (Oxford: Osprey Publishing, 2010).

MAGAZINES, JOURNALS, AND NEWS PAPER ARTICLES

Clementson, John, "Strike and Support 'Nusoor Oman' The Sultan of Oman's Airforce in the Dhofar War", The Journal of the Sultan's Armed Forces Association, 2003, Issue 52.

Hughes, Dr Geraint, All the Shah's Men: The Imperial Iranian Brigade Group in the Dhofar War. King's College Research Centre for the History of Conflict, 6 June 2016.

Monick, S. Victory in Hades: The Forgotten Wars of the Oman 1957-1959 and 1970-1976 Part 1, Scientia Militaria, South African Journal of Military Studies, Vol 12, Nr 3, 1982.

Monick, S. Victory in Hades: The Forgotten Wars of the Oman 1957-1959 and 1970-1976 Part 2, Scientia Militaria, South African Journal of Military Studies, Vol 12, Nr 4, 1982.

Monick, S. Victory in Hades: The Forgotten Wars of the Oman 1957-1959 and 1970-1976 Part 2, Scientia Militaria, South African Journal of Military Studies, Vol 13, Nr 1, 1983.

Schade, Alexander, Counterinsurgency Strategy in the Dhofar Rebellion, Small Wars Journal and Military Writers Guild Writing Contest Finalist Article, Journal Article, 20 April 2017.

Smiley, David "Oman 1958-1961", The Journal of the Sultan's Armed Forces Association, Issue 50, 2001.

Pace, Eric "Shah of Iran Uses Oman to Train Armed Forces", The New York Times, 25 January 1976.

Wynn, Humphrey, Sultan's Airforce, Flight International, 5 July 1971.

UNPUBLISHED UNIT HISTORIES AND NOTES

Baird, Brig. J.E.A. CBE, Various Papers re typed by Nora Baird Campbell.

Bowes, Berty, Notes on the Muscat Regiment 1961-1962.

Friedberger, John, The Northern Frontier Regiment.

Guide to British Troops entering Oman – 1960.

Instrs for Br Seconded Offrs joining SAF 1961.

The Signal Regiment Past and Present, Oman Signal Regiment, 1982.

The Formation and Early Years of the Muscat Levy Corps, Later the Muscat Infantry. Records of Oman Archive Editions, Vol III Chapter 13, 1988.

ONLINE

Arabian Aerospace Online News Service, "Small air force with a big reputation", https://www.arabianaerospace.aero/small-air-force-with-a-big-reputation.html, 21 December 2011.

Imran Shamsunahar, "The Dhofar war and the myth of localized conflicts", Real Clear Defense, https://www.realcleardefense.com/articles/2018/01/12/.

Robert G. Landen, Anglo–Omani Treaties. Encyclopaedia of the Modern Middle East and North Africa. Encyclopedia.com. 23 Jan. 2019. https://www.encyclopedia.com.

Sultan's Armed Forces Association web site and Journals, https://www.oman.org.uk/ (diverse issues).

CORRESPONDENCE

Tom Wylie Ulster Museum; Lt Col Peter Wilson REME (British Loan Service Advisor to Head of EME RAO); Brig Halfan Hamed Al-Sulaimani; Ameed Rukn (engineer); Mohammed Ahmed Al Lamki Commander SAF Signals; Commander Khalid bin Khalfan bin Ali Al Maqbali (Staff Officer 1 Coordination and following up Office of Commander of the Royal Navy of Oman); Capt Charles Butt (SAF and Aden Protectorate Levies) Maj M.R. Adams (SAF Signal Regt MAM); Muqaddam MEG Chandler (SAF Signal Regiment); Maj M.S. Wilson-Brown (HQ SAF Signals)

EMAIL CORRESPONDENCE

Dr Athol Yates; Dr Aaron Fox; Dr James Onley (CD FRHistS FRAS Institute of Arab & Islamic Studies University of Exeter); Muqaddam Ian Buttenshaw (Royal Army of Oman Historian); Maj Eddie Parks (SOA SAF); Catherine Lord; Stephen Lord; Harry Pugh; Owain Raw-Rees; Ali Al-Shahwani; Graham Wheeldon; Steve Rothwell; Pipe Major Gavin Moffat (O.C. Oman 3 RG Band Sqn); Peter Shaw; Alastair MacDonald and Marc Sherriff.

MUSEUMS & INSTITUTIONS

The National Archives UK, National Archives Australia, SAF Museum Muscat Oman, Khalifa University Abu Dhabi, Imperial War Museum UK.

ABOUT THE AUTHOR

Cliff Lord served in Britain's Royal Signals during the 1960s as a cipher operator in England, Germany and on active service in Aden and the East Aden Protectorate. Following his military service, Cliff worked in Paris for the Washington Post and later moved to New Zealand working as a computer operator, a communications network controller for Air New Zealand and Team Leader International Operations for the Southern Cross fibre optics trans pacific cable before retiring. He is Honorary Historian for Royal New Zealand Corps of Signals. Cliff has written twelve books, including this one, on military history including SIGINT, and insignia, and this is his second instalment for Helion's @War series.